Praise for *Seekii*

This beautifully written memoir is rich in particulars from the author's girlhood in wartime Britain, giving us not just the sound of rockets and air raid sirens, the sight of bombed-out buildings, but also the smells and tastes of ration-era recipes, instructions for constructing and sleeping in home-built shelters, and an unexpected use for a gas mask. The narrative is sharp-eyed and fiercely honest, funny and heartbreaking, full of complex individuals responding to the hardships and dangers and occasional pleasures of civilian life in time of war, a life further complicated for the author and her family by intergenerational conflicts, class prejudice, and antisemitism. *Seeking Shelter* is an education and a delight.

—**Lon Otto**, author of *The Flower Trade* and *A Man in Trouble: Stories*

One expects a memoir of a childhood in wartime Britain to be told from the perspective of an adult looking back, reflecting, analyzing, and drawing parallels to our own era. Instead, Cynthia Ehrenkrantz writes as the child she was in those years – astute, aware, curious, precociously literate, always eavesdropping on adults, constantly processing what goes on around her. In *Seeking Shelter*, she deftly weaves two tales together: an invaluable account of the realities of World War II as British civilians lived it every day, and the personal story of a British-Jewish family struggling to survive while worrying over the fate of relatives in Europe whose voices have gone ominously dark. Her recall is astounding, and her skill at telling her story from the perspective of a child transitioning to preadolescence takes readers on a fascinating journey of maturation.

—**Rabbi Lester Bronstein,** Bet Am Shalom Synagogue, White Plains, NY

Seeking Shelter transported me to a time and place I'd learned about as history: Britain during WWII. In her new memoir, Cynthia Ehrenkrantz brings that history to life through the experiences of a Jewish child growing up in wartime England. Writing in vivid and intimate detail, she allows us to see what she saw, feel what she felt and share her thoughts, hopes and dreams. We learn that while her world was often confusing, lonely and scary, it was also filled with warmth and small pleasures, childhood adventures and colorful people. This book was a joy to read and is a must-read for anyone interested in understanding the personal side of historical events.

—**Karen Gershowitz**, author of *Travel Mania: Stories of Wanderlust*

Seeking Shelter

Memoir of a Jewish Girlhood in Wartime Britain

by
Cynthia Ehrenkrantz

Library of Congress Control Number (in progress)

Cover design: JT Lindroos

Formatted, Converted, and Distributed by eBookIt.com
http://www.eBookIt.com

ISBN-13: 978-1-4566-3912-9 (paperback)
ISBN-13: 978-1-4566-3914-3 (ebook)

Dedication

To Ruth, Dan and Jonathan

Epigraph

When I lie where shades of darkness
Shall no more assail mine eyes,
Nor the rain make lamentation
When the wind sighs;
How will fare the world whose wonder
Was the very proof of me?
Memory fades, must the remembered
Perishing be?

—**Walter de la Mare**, "Fare Well"

War is very cruel. It goes on for so long.
—**Winston Churchill**

Author's Note

I never meant to write a memoir about growing up in Britain during World War II, but *Seeking Shelter* grew into one whether I intended it or not.

Many years ago, I decided to record my early memories in order to leave these stories for my children. I sensed that, if I didn't, a time might come when they would regret not asking me about my history, just as I have come to regret not learning more about my own parents' early years.

The events recorded here are as I remember them, with facts, dates and places verified where possible. Another person living through the same experiences might recall them differently. All memory is subjective. I can only say I have tried to make this account of my own experiences accurate and truthful.

Names of family members, friends, teachers and other people mentioned in this memoir are mostly real. A few names have been changed intentionally or approximate names I can't recall.

With one exception (Lord Woolton Pie), the recipes are also drawn from memory. I include them to give readers a sense of how families ate during wartime and encourage anyone interested in trying them to look for variations online.

CONTENTS

Prologue: Tilly and Max

The postcard read:

Dear Tilly,
   Please come to tea on Sunday, July 12th at
4:00 o'clock. My cousin Max Shelower is going
to be here, and I'd like you to meet him.
                                    Kind regards,
                                        Malka

No doubt her mother had been complaining to cousin Malka again, Tilly thought: "Find someone for my Tilly. She's twenty-five already."

Tilly had no intention of remaining single, but so far hadn't found anyone she could consider marrying. She'd dated Jack Friedberg for almost a year. He was blond, nice looking and a good dancer. They'd even won a Charleston contest. But when he proposed, she turned him down. He was so dull. A tailor like her father and brothers, his conversation was mundane, his accent low class. She couldn't imagine settling down with him.

Tilly's mother, Rivke, berated her. "He's steady. A good provider. You're too fussy. You'll be left on the shelf like your sisters."

Tilly was one of five full siblings, the children of her father Shlomo Fox's third marriage. His first two wives had died in childbirth after bearing three sons and a daughter between them—Tilly's older half-sibilings Hersch Meyer, Victor, Shmuel and Betsy. Her half-siblings were all married but she and her full siblings—her sisters Milly, Rose and Fan and her brother, Goody—were still single and living at home in North London, much to their widowed mother's disappointment.

Like his three half-brothers, Goody owned a successful tailoring and furrier store. Rose worked with Goody. She was shy, never knowing what to say to men, always looking down at her hands in her lap and blushing. Fan, a dressmaker, had had a boyfriend, but he'd gone to Argentina five years before to seek his fortune, promising to send for her when he'd saved enough money. At first, he'd written weekly, then once a month. After three years, his letters stopped and Fan lost hope. Milly, the youngest sister, was a hairdresser and was considered "fast." She was still "playing the field" and had many boyfriends. Tilly was a milliner and talented amateur actress. She planned to marry eventually but not until she found the right man.

Tilly got off the bus when it reached Stamford Hill, and walked up Olinda Road past identical Victorian row houses to number 68. It was a sunny day in July 1931 and she was wearing a dusty-pink dress falling just below her knees, the belt fastener made of two silver pelicans with interlocking beaks. She'd made the cloche hat herself to match the dress perfectly, staying after her shift in the millinery workshop, stretching and steaming the felt on a wooden mold so it fit just right. She knew she looked chic.

Malka greeted her with a swift kiss on the cheek and ushered her into the dining room. The table was overflowing with teatime delicacies: smoked salmon, pickled and chopped herring, crisp celery sticks, pickled cabbage, caraway-seeded rye bread, sweet butter and a big wedge of cheddar cheese.

As Tilly entered, a young man unfolded his lanky frame from a chair, and when he stood she saw he was quite a bit taller than she was. A plus, she thought. At five foot eight, she was often introduced to young men who were shorter; many tended to plumpness, which she found most unattractive. Max was tall and slim with broad shoulders, and his horn-rimmed glasses gave him a studious air. When he offered his hand, she noticed how the corners of his eyes crinkled when he smiled. His voice when he introduced himself was a deep, resonant bass. He was dressed in the latest fashion: Oxford bags—baggy trousers with legs so wide they looked almost like two long skirts.

"Max has come up from Wales on a buying trip," Malka said.

"I do the purchasing for my father's wallpaper shop," Max explained in a strong Welsh accent. The shop, named Papertones, was in Merthyr Tydfil, a Welsh market town. "I come up to London about every six weeks," he added. Tilly noticed he had a slight lisp. A pity, she thought, because he seemed interesting.

Later, when he walked her to the bus stop, he asked, "Do you like classical music?"

"Why, yes. I've been to the opera and loved it," she said.

"There's a piano recital at the Courtauld Institute on Tuesday evening. Would you like to come?"

Tilly accepted, feeling a little thrill of excitement.

Years later, Max would tell Tilly he'd accepted Malka's invitation to meet "a nice Jewish girl" with little enthusiasm, expecting to meet some swarthy-skinned young woman with "frizzy hair and piano legs." But Tilly was tall and willowy with high, Slavic cheekbones, deep blue eyes and an alabaster complexion.

Tilly quickly learned that, unlike her previous suitors, Max wasn't at all dull. He played the piano and violin, and obviously came from a well-to-do family. Like Tilly, he read voraciously and loved classical music. On their first date, they discovered they both admired the work of H.G. Wells and J.B. Priestley and that their politics mutually leaned to the left.

They discovered they also had the same amount of schooling, both having left school at age 14. Max had been a poor student due to undiagnosed dyslexia. When he left school, he went to work in his father's wallpaper store. He confided to Tilly that he was concerned about the family business. Most of their customers were miners and their house-proud wives, he explained. During the course of a year, their houses would get covered in coal dust, and they liked to spruce things up with whitewash every spring. "I don't know what's going to happen now unemployment allowances have been reduced," Max said. "I'm afraid they won't be able to afford to paint next year."

Tilly nodded in sympathy. "Did you read about this man Oswald Mosley and his Blackshirts?" she asked.

"I certainly did. They want to deport all the Jews. Let's hope they don't draw any followers."

Unlike Max, Tilly had been an excellent student, so good that she had been offered a scholarship to a private school at age 11. But, like many Orthodox Jews, her parents were suspicious of secular education. They had been horrified when neighbors' children came home from college and mocked their parents' religious practices, calling them silly superstitions. Worried that Tilly would get "too big for her boots" if she went to a private school, they kept her in the local elementary school where she spent her last year as a teacher's aide, tutoring younger children.

"You'll learn a trade," her father said. "With a trade in your two hands you'll always be able to earn a living." A week after leaving school, she had begun a seven-year apprenticeship as a milliner. She was working full-time when she met Max while also pursuing her love of acting. As soon as she started work, she began saving her weekly allowance, walking to scrimp on bus fare and packing sandwiches for lunch, until she had enough to apply to a drama school attached to the Q Theatre. Most of her evenings were spent there, and by the time she met Max she had already starred in productions of *The Last of Mrs. Cheyney* and George Bernard Shaw's *The Devil's Disciple*. Her life was full and happy and she saw no reason to change it... yet.

Their courtship was long distance. They wrote letters, Max's becoming warmer and more affectionate as time went by, telling Tilly how much he missed her. Tilly was careful to maintain a demure tone, not wanting to appear too eager. As Max pronounced his name in a thick Welsh accent it sounded more like Marcus, and she decided to call him that. The name was quite distinguished, she thought. More Anglicized.

On their third date, he asked her to come with him to his tailor. Tilly was impressed when they entered a hushed Saville Row establishment with coats of arms discreetly displayed on the door. She noted that members of the royal family shopped there. Tilly helped him select fabric for two suits: a finely woven navy blue pinstripe and a brown Harris tweed. Then she watched while the tailor whipped out his tape measure and deftly wound it around Max's upper arms and waist. She began to view Max as a catch.

When they'd been seeing each other for a couple of months, he invited her to Merthyr to meet his family. Tilly was dazzled by the grand house, opulently furnished with antiques, an upright piano, a real bearskin rug and a French ormolu clock in the parlor.

Max's parents, Polish Jews like her own, spoke terrible broken English, worse than Tilly's mother. One afternoon, Max's mother invited Tilly to go shopping. "You vant to come mit?" she asked. Tilly smiled at the comical blend of English and Yiddish.

"You mean 'come with me,'" Tilly said, correcting Mrs. Shelower as she would have done with her own mother.

"Don't tell me how to speak de English," Polly Shelower said sharply. "Who's been here longer you *tse* me?"

At breakfast on Saturday morning, Max's father was glowering as he waved a piece of paper under Max's nose. "Maax. Vat is dis?"

"Oh yes. That must be the bill from the tailor," Max replied.

"How many times do I have to tell you?" Barney Shelower shouted, banging his fist on the table. "You buy expensive suits ven you earn enough money to pay for dem yourself. Dis is de last time I pay dis kind of a bill."

Max shrugged and winked at Tilly over his father's head. She felt a twinge of discomfort being privy to a family argument that was, apparently, longstanding.

On Sunday morning, Max stood at the top of the stairs after his bath, clad in a dressing gown, and called down to his youngest sister: "Nellie! Where's my underwear? Nellie! Where's my shirt?"

Tilly watched as 18-year-old Nellie ran up and down the stairs, catering to her brother's needs. Tilly made a mental note: if they got married, she would never let him order her about like that.

Nellie was the more gregarious of Max's two sisters. Her cheerful personality, good head for business and strong design sense made her an asset to Max's father at the store. Dolly, 23, was a talented musician and painter. She helped her mother with cooking and housekeeping and sometimes worked in the shop, but she had no interest in any of it, preferring to spend her time at the piano or her easel.

The wedding was on March 28, 1932. Max's wedding present to Tilly was a Cocker Spaniel mix puppy. He loved dogs and, although Tilly had only had cats before, she soon grew fond of the puppy she named Judy.

They looked for a place to open their own paint and wallpaper shop and decided on Croydon, a South London suburb where a number of large factories and Britain's busy main airport, Croydon Aerodrome, were located. Max was impressed by the dense crowds of shoppers in town on the Saturday he and Tilly visited—so many, they spilled off the sidewalk onto the road.

"This town is good for business," he said, so they found retail space on London Road, where they opened Walltones, a shop like his father's. Max and Tilly moved into the flat above the store and planned to save for the down payment on a house. Tilly gave up acting to help Max run the business.

They intended to wait a couple of years before starting a family but nature took its course and I was born one year and sixteen days after the wedding.

PART ONE:
A CROYDON CHILDHOOD

Chapter 1
Praying for Curls

T he poor man hanging on the silver cross attached to
Mother Patricia's belt looked so sad. His arms were
stretched out sideways, the hands drooping, his head
lolling to one side. All the girls lined up in front of our black-
robed teacher and took turns kissing him. I thought
everyone was kissing him to make him feel better.

When I reached the front of the line, I leaned forward to
do the same.

Mother Patricia said, "No, no, Cynthia. You don't have
to kiss the crucifix. You're Jewish. Just go and sit in the circle
with the other girls." It was my first day at Coloma Convent.
I wondered if the sad man minded my not kissing him.

I was three years old and too young for kindergarten but
my parents had wanted me to start school because my
mother was working extended hours at Walltones, my
parents' paint and wallpaper store.. It was 1936. England
was still mired in the Great Depression, and they were
struggling to make a living. There was so little business that
my father had let go of Sam, his only employee, because he
couldn't afford to pay Sam's salary of four pounds a week—
about $400 today.

My mother, of course, would work in the store without
pay.

Nursery schools were virtually unknown in England at
the time, but Coloma Convent was a couple of blocks from

our house, making it easy for Mummy to drop me off each morning before work.

I was the first grandchild on either side of the family, slender and tall for my age, surrounded on my mother's side by a doting grandmother, three aunts and an uncle whom we visited often in North London and who hung on my every word. They all thought I was some kind of wunderkind, and their undivided attention encouraged my precociousness. My mother took me to Coloma for an interview and I was accepted, though I was two years younger than my classmates.

We were typical British Jews. My parents kept a kosher home, and my mother lit candles every Friday night to welcome the Sabbath, when my father recited prayers over bread and wine. We went to synagogue three times a year: on the two days of Rosh Hashanah, the Jewish New Year; and on Yom Kippur, the Day of Atonement. Confident that my Jewish identity was well established, my parents were unconcerned about my attending a Catholic school run by nuns. In England, with no separation between church and state, all schools were affiliated with a church anyway. What did it matter if the other girls prayed to "Our Father, Who art in heaven" or recited *Ave Maria*? As a Jewish child, I would be excused from all prayers and religious instruction. I started school with great excitement.

The nuns at Coloma were sweet and kind. We called Mother Benignus, the lower school principal, Old Mother Big Knickers, and although I'm sure she overheard us we were never reprimanded.

Kindergarten was a wonderland where I threw myself into activities with great enthusiasm. We played in a Wendy House with a wooden frame and flimsy cloth walls printed in a brick pattern to resemble the house described in *Peter*

Pan. Once a week, I helped make a gelatin dessert to serve at lunchtime. The nuns taught us how to pour boiling water from a teakettle so it didn't splash onto the cubes of gelatin or on us, stirring the mixture carefully until it dissolved. When we were lunch monitors, we put on lace caps and aprons—just like real waitresses—and carefully carried dishes of the jewel-colored dessert to our classmates. I loved the way it shimmered and trembled on the plate. We learned how to embroider, and I mastered the intricacies of chain stitch, stem stitch and lazy daisy, and made myself my very own pencil case decorated with flowers.

Twice a week, the other girls filed out to study Catechism in the chapel. When I tried to follow them, Mother Patricia made me stay behind in our cheery classroom, where I occupied myself with crayons and the toy kitchen. When the class learned Christmas carols, Mother Patricia said I could go play in the Wendy House. But the tunes were so lilting and the words so appealing I learned them anyway: "Away in a manger, no crib for a bed, the little Lord Jesus lay down his sweet head...."

For the school concert at the end of the year, we were asked which nursery rhyme we would like to perform. To Mother Patricia's consternation, I chose "Hot Cross Buns," a rhyme about a traditional Easter confection. She tried in vain to make me choose something else, suggesting "Mary Had a Little Lamb" or "Mary, Mary, Quite Contrary," but I was adamant. "Hot Cross Buns" was my favorite. Auntie Fan made me a dress of beige iridescent satin with puffy rosettes on the skirt that looked something like cakes. She drew the line at embroidering crosses on the bodice however, which the pattern suggested.

I sang my song loud and clear, waving wildly at the finish, pointing to the back of the hall, and calling out in a booming voice, "There's my mummy and daddy!" I was thrilled when the audience laughed and applauded. Too young to know anything about my mother's theatrical background, at my first public performance I made up my mind: I was going to be an actress.

Shirley Temple was the most popular film star of the day, and my adoring aunts took me to all her movies. I would sit in my seat, licking an ice cream cone, gazing up at the screen amid a huge audience of admiring little girls. We all longed to look like Shirley. My mother bought me polka dot dresses with smocking across the bodice and matching panties, just like the ones Shirley wore in *Stand Up and Cheer!* I tried to make dimples like hers by poking my cheeks with a sharp pencil, but I only succeeded in creating sore red patches. "Stop doing that," Mummy reprimanded. "You'll give yourself lead poisoning."

I practiced tap dancing in the living room. Behind one of the floor-length brown velvet drapes was a box attached to the wall encasing the telephone connection, its wires snaking down the wall and along the baseboard. I hid behind the curtain pretending the outlet was a microphone, singing "On the Good Ship Lollipop." I hoped, if I practiced enough, someone from Hollywood would discover me and I would join Shirley, perhaps as her sidekick or best friend.

Shirley had something no amount of money could buy: a head of thick, blond ringlets. My wispy, straight, mouse-brown hair bore no resemblance to her curly mop.

"Don't worry," Auntie Rose said. "When you're grown up you can get a permanent wave." But grown up seemed so far away. I couldn't wait that long.

One day, my mother came home and pulled something out of her shopping basket that looked like a tube of toothpaste. "Look what I've found," she said. "It's called

Curly Top and they say it can make straight hair curly." She combed the sticky gel into my wet hair and tried to make curls around her finger. But as soon as it dried, my hair drooped back, straight as a broomstick. Such hair would never make it to Hollywood. *All* the child stars had curls.

When I was five, I'd been in kindergarten for nearly two years and was allowed to walk the two blocks home from school by myself. I had a flash of inspiration one day: I would perform a penance to earn the curls I deserved. I stood outside Coloma Convent, put my hands together, closed my eyes and prayed aloud: "Dear God, if you will only let me have curly hair, I will pretend to be blind all the way home to my house. Please, please answer my prayer. Amen."

I shut my eyes tight, placed my hand on the brick wall outside the school and, walking sideways like a crab, groped along prickly hedges and splintery fences, praying all the way. "Dear God, I am doing this penance for you. Please, please, God, let me have curly hair."

I heard a woman say, "Whatever is the matter with that child?" But the English are naturally reserved and no one asked me directly what I was doing.

After what seemed like hours, I felt the familiar wooden fence outside our house. I unlatched the gate and carefully put one foot in front of the other, feeling my way up the path to the front door, which I opened with my own key. Inside, keeping my eyes closed, I followed the banister upstairs to the bathroom. At last, I opened my eyes and looked in the mirror.

My hair was as straight as ever. What kind of a cruel God would disappoint me so callously?

I was six when my mother found me genuflecting in front of the telephone outlet and decided for reasons I did not yet understand that it was time for me to leave Coloma Convent Girls' School.

Determined not to send me to a state school, Mummy found a small private institution, Miss Cleal's Academy, run by two genteel spinster sisters out of their Victorian home. They organized it like a one-room schoolhouse with pupils ranging in age from five to twelve. We met around a large dining table and spent recess playing on the lawn in the large backyard. We memorized poems and practiced cursive writing, laboriously copying curly, copperplate letters into our exercise books. I was happy at Miss Cleal's School, completely content with my life, too young and innocent to think anything would ever change.

Chapter 2
Bubbe's House

O n most weekends, we went to visit my mother's family in North London. Her mother, my *bubbe*, lived at 77 Devonshire Road in the commuter suburb of Palmers Green. Devonshire Road houses were identical: Victorian, semi-detached, red brick structures with tiled paths bordered by standard rose bushes leading to their front doors.

I loved going to Bubbe's house. I skipped up the street from the bus stop, lifted the latch on the garden gate, jumped onto the front step and banged the shiny brass doorknocker. The front door rattled and I heard Bubbe's thudding footfall as she ran to greet us down the long narrow hallway she called "the passage." She hugged me so tight I could feel the whalebones in her corset as I buried my face in her ample belly. "*Mein einekl. Azoy zees,*" she said in Yiddish. *My grandchild. So sweet.*

We hung our coats on the ornately carved hallstand. My mother took off her hat and combed her hair, glancing into the beveled mirror. Light coming through the stained glass panels in the front door threw blue and red patterns on the walls and floor. As I walked toward the eat-in kitchen, I ran my hand over embossed Lincrusta wallpaper with its elaborate design of intertwined roses. Tea and *kichel* – cookies sprinkled with cinnamon and sugar – were always waiting for us in the kitchen, and Bubbe always encouraged me to eat more.

"You're such a skinny *galina*," she said. "Eat, eat, *mamaleh.*"

Bubbe wasn't tall but she was wide. In the mornings, she came downstairs wearing a dark-colored dress reaching almost to her ankles. Peering into the mirror over the fireplace with her light blue eyes, looking at her reflection, she always muttered, "Isn't it awful?" as if she was expecting to see a much younger woman. She twisted her white hair into a bun and poked hairpins into it. Then she sat on a kitchen chair and wound crepe bandages around heavy legs covered with the worst varicose veins I had ever seen. Finally, she pulled on thick lisle stockings and slipped her feet into lumpy shoes. "*Oy, mein feese,*" she'd complain as her aching, buniony feet hit the kitchen floor. Now she was ready for the day.

My maiden aunts Rose, Milly and Fan lived in Bubbe's house along with my bachelor Uncle Goody. Bubbe ruled the roost, mostly from the kitchen, where she prepared two meals a day without fail for anyone who needed feeding.

Bubbe made me all kinds of special treats: golden syrup-flavored semolina and vanilla pudding served in a huge Victorian mug decorated with beautiful purple grapes. Eggs delicately scrambled with onions and tomatoes and seasoned liberally with white pepper. Family meals consisted of hearty soups, thick with barley or potatoes. On Saturdays, we ate small portions of meat or chicken served with boiled cabbage. I loved my grandmother's cooking.

My great-grandfather, Bubbe's father, Herschl Krycer, had been a baker in Poland, and she had started working alongside him when she was 12, weighing the dough for loaves of bread. When she was 13, she was sent to work for innkeeper cousins. In their kitchen, she learned how to prepare salty snacks and pickles to put on the bar. Free, salty things made customers thirsty so they ordered more beer. In 1898, when she married my grandfather, Shlomo Fox, at the age of 18 and emigrated with him to England, she was already an experienced cook. Everything was measured out in her hand and by eye and all her recipes were in her head.

While she cooked, she sang Yiddish songs from her girlhood in Poland and tunes her stepsons brought home from the London music halls. These became a garbled mishmash of Yiddish and English interspersed with "deedle deedle dum." A verse to one of her favorites, "Darling Mabel," began:

> *Darling Mabel,*
> *Now I'm able*
> *To buy this happy home....*

But Bubbe's version was:

> *Darling Mabel,*
> *Bought a table,*
> *Half a dozen chairs.*
> *First she vashed 'em. Den she scrubbed 'em.*
> *Deedle deedle dum.*

When Bubbe wasn't singing the words, she hummed as she worked, and I sang along with her.

Bubbe had no fancy kitchen. She worked in the scullery, a drafty, dimly lit afterthought of a room, with an uneven floor paved with pitted, ice-cold, terra cotta tiles. Her equipment consisted of a sink with a wooden draining board, a small gas stove and a freestanding cabinet for storing pots and skillets. Out of this dingy room came shoals of golden fried fish, fragrant gleaming challahs, poached carp in a spicy jelled sauce, barrels of pickled red and white cabbage, marinated herring and great simmering pots of comforting soups. Her ingredients were simple: cabbage, onions, cucumbers, potatoes and flour. We ate these delicious meals in the adjoining eat-in kitchen.

In late summer, when fresh peas grew fat and hard in the pod, I would help her shell them to make one of my favorite soups: peas with *kliskalach*. First I shelled the peas and Bubbe boiled the empty peapods to make a vegetable stock. Then I helped her make the kliskalach—little egg noodles made by adding flour and seasonings to a beaten egg until it became a stiff dough. It was my job to break off tiny, pea-sized pieces of dough and spread them on a board to dry. The resulting soup was a magic bowlful of peas that popped in your mouth and chewy, miniature dumplings in a spicy, delicate broth.

Foods that needed to be kept cold were stored on a tiled shelf in the larder, a storage cabinet vented to the outside. Without refrigeration, milk often went sour in the summer heat, and when it did, Bubbe made cream cheese. She waited until the milk, delivered in glass bottles every day, was completely curdled. Then she tipped the curds into a cheesecloth bag to hang from the kitchen faucet overnight, allowing the whey to drip into the sink. In the morning, she removed the drained curds, mixed them with salt and the cream that had risen to the top of fresh milk, then mixed the cheese with slivers of green onions and radishes to be spread on slices of rye bread and home-baked challah.

In Bubbe's house, when guests dropped by on Saturday afternoons, they were invited to sit around a table laden with chopped and pickled herring, celery sticks standing upright in a cut glass vase, dilled cucumbers, pickled red and white cabbage, and homemade cream cheese.

While the rest of my mother's family had strayed from strict Orthodox Judaism, Bubbe remained observant. No cooking was done on Saturdays. It was, she told me, a day to "sleep in," and so, when we visited, I climbed into bed with her on Saturday mornings to cuddle up and luxuriate under the down comforter she'd brought with her from Poland as a bride. Her Edwardian wardrobe was carved with grinning gargoyles and roses. My mother and aunts thought they were hideous but Bubbe loved this piece of furniture, handmade by a cabinetmaker friend of the family when my grandparents first arrived in England. As I lay in her bed, I peeped between my fingers at the ornate animals who seemed to move and bare their teeth at me—magical and a little scary.

When I stayed at Bubbe's house I spent most days in my Uncle Goody's shop on the main street in Palmers Green. The sign over the shop window read: Goodwin Fox, Tailor and Furrier. Auntie Rose and Uncle Goody worked together as a team, sitting on wooden tailor stools making classic suits and coats for their clientele. The clothes looked exactly the same year after year. Goody's only nod to fashion was to raise or lower hemlines. Those frumpy clothes were popular with the local matrons, who came back every year, developing warm friendships with my aunt and uncle.

They found lots of jobs for me: sorting buttons or reels of thread; crawling under the table to pick up dropped pins with a horseshoe-shaped magnet; pulling out white basting stitches after garments had been sewn together.... While they worked, Goody and Rose joined in the choruses of popular songs playing on the radio. "A Tisket a Tasket" and "You Must Have Been a Beautiful Baby" were favorites.

Above the store, a second sign swung outside an upstairs window: Francine, Dressmaker. Upstairs, Auntie Fan made clothes for the same clientele. She specialized in formal dresses decorated with tiny beads in elaborate floral designs sewn onto collars, cuffs, and bodices—dresses to be worn to weddings and bar mitzvahs. Her workroom was decorated with prints of flowers, and her collection of Royal Doulton figurines stood on the mantel next to a photograph of a handsome man. When I asked who he was, Auntie Fan said he was a good friend who had moved to Argentina.

My three aunts all competed for my attention. Auntie Milly took me to movies and knitted me sweaters. Fan made clothes for my dolls and for me, and Rose took me to Kew Gardens when the rhododendrons were in bloom. But the best treats of all came from Uncle Goody.

Goodwin Fox, my grandmother's only son, was good in name and good by nature. In 1929, my grandfather was hit by a car when crossing the street. In hospital, he fell on his way to the bathroom and died, probably from a stroke. Goody was 26 when his father died, and he supported my grandmother financially from that day on. He was a brilliant man who went to work cheerfully every day, even though he had no love for tailoring. Surrounded by a gaggle of women who adored him, he was witty, well-read and wise. Once a year, in December, Uncle Goody took a whole day off work to treat me to lunch in an American-style restaurant, where I feasted on waffles and ice cream. In the afternoon, we watched cartoons in a movie theater. Then, after a lavish tea with chocolate eclairs and cream puffs in Lyons Corner House, we attended a traditional holiday-season Pantomime, where we watched well-known comedians in drag play the Dame and female musical comedy stars clad in tights and teeny mini-skirts sing popular songs. Pantomimes always included sing-alongs with the audience, with everyone making the same gestures to accompany certain words in the song—spreading our arms wide, pointing to a person near us, touching our heads, clasping our hands to our chests…. I enjoyed watching Uncle Goody singing and messing up the silly gestures almost as much as I enjoyed the performance.

Sticky and tired, I would fall asleep on the bus back to Palmers Green until Uncle Goody shook me awake for the short walk home to Bubbe's house. My mother would tuck me into bed, and I'd drift off to sleep, imagining myself clad in tights and singing my heart out on the stage.

Peas and Kliskalach Soup

Peas
- 2 pounds English peas in the shell
- 2 large onions, diced
- 3 ounces margarine or butter
- 6 cups water
- 1 tablespoon sugar

Kliskalach
- 1 egg
- ½ cup flour
- 1/8 teaspoon powdered ginger
- Salt
- White pepper

1. Beat the egg together with the ginger, salt and pepper. Add enough flour while beating to make a stiff dough.
2. Pinch off little pieces of dough and roll them between your finger and thumb. Place them on a flat surface to dry.
3. While the kliskalach are drying shell the peas and set aside.
4. Put the empty pods in a pot of water. Bring to a boil, then turn down heat and simmer until the pods are very soft. Discard the pods.

5. Add the peas and kliskalach to the pod-water together with sugar, pepper and salt and simmer. Don't worry if the peas seem to overcook. They will release their flavor into the soup in the process.

6. While the peas are cooking, sauté the onions in the margarine until they are soft and translucent.

7. Add the onions to the soup and season well with salt and white pepper. Taste for seasoning. The soup should have a slight "bite" from the pepper balanced by sweetness from the peas and sugar.

Chapter 3
Sewing Circle

*I*n November 1938, soon after Kristallnacht (The Night of Broken Glass), members of Britain's Jewish community met with Prime Minister Neville Chamberlain to discuss a report a Quaker mission had prepared on the events of that night. They appealed to him to make it easier to bring Jewish children to Britain, but he refused. A few days later, a joint delegation of Quakers and members of the Jewish community appealed more successfully to the Home Secretary, Samuel Hoare, who came from a Quaker family, and the government finally agreed to allow unaccompanied Jewish refugee children under age 17 to enter the country from Germany, Austria, Czechoslovakia, and Poland. Refugee agencies had to promise to fully finance and organize the operation and also pay for the children's eventual return home. To support the program, which became known as the Kindertransport, the Jewish community, along with other non-Jewish groups, guaranteed funding of 50 pounds per child—about $4,700 today.

On a rainy afternoon the following May, my mother and I walked up the front steps of a big house.

"Hold on to the banister, Cynthia," she said. "The steps might be slippery from the rain. Let me hold Brenda for you." I passed my doll to her.

A hand-shaped brass knocker with the index finger pointing downward gleamed on the front door. My mother tapped it gently and the door was opened by a woman with faded blonde braids twisted around her head.

"Come in please," she said in a heavy foreign accent.

We entered a small foyer where a coat tree already held several drippy raincoats. A stuffed umbrella stand stood in the corner and a spindly-legged table supported a spiky-leafed plant in a mottled, dark green pot. A whiff of boiling cabbage wafted from the back of the house.

"I am Mrs. Gerhardt, ze house muzzer for ze boys," the woman said, ushering us toward a murmur of female voices. We entered a room where several women sat around a long, oval table covered with a plush, dark red tablecloth. The women had sewing boxes in front of them. My mother pulled hers from a carry-all and splayed it open, revealing three trays on each side holding neatly arranged needle cases, thread, scissors, thimbles and a red pincushion in the shape of a tomato. At home, I loved playing with the box.

"Hello, Tilly. Come and sit next to me," my mother's friend Betty Young said, moving her chair to make room. She pointed to a big armchair. "Here's a chair for you, Cynthia. Did you bring something to play with?"

"I brought a book to read to Brenda," I said.

Brenda, my constant companion, wasn't like other dolls. For one thing, her eyes were brown, not blue; and not only did they open and close, they moved from side to side like magic. The size of a newborn baby, she wore my old baby clothes. My mother pulled A.A. Milne's *Now We Are Six* from her handbag. Auntie Rose had given it to me for my sixth birthday the previous month. I loved the poems, particularly "Binker," about an imaginary friend. My imaginary friend was named Jonathan.

Brenda's clothes had become damp from drizzle on our way from the bus stop, so I took them off and spread them on the arm of the chair to dry. An afghan hung over the back of the armchair and I covered her with it so she wouldn't catch cold. Then I opened the book and glanced at the familiar poems, but after a few minutes I put it aside. Listening to the women around the table was more interesting.

"Pass me another sock," Betty Young said. "These boys go through them so fast. I'd swear I darned this one last week."

"We should probably set up a kitty to buy them new clothes," Becky Cowan said. "They're growing boys, and these aren't going to last them very long."

"They've cost us a lot already," my mother said. "The government asked for fifty pounds apiece to bring them into the country and now you want to ask for more money? They're like a bottomless pit. "

"Come on now, Tilly," Becky said. "Think of what they were facing at home. The boys in this house all have fathers in those work camps. Some of the older ones were in the camps themselves. Germany seems to be going mad, relocating people willy-nilly, smashing shop windows, burning books."

"Yes," my mother said. "We wrote to our cousins in Poland recommending they leave the country and go to Australia, where we have family. But they wrote back saying it would all blow over soon. Their business is doing so well, we couldn't persuade them."

"It's too bad they can't come here," Kit Sabel said. "But the Kindertransport only takes children under seventeen."

"My brother, Goody, sponsored an older German refugee," my mother said. "You're allowed to do that if you can guarantee them employment and a place to live. She's living in my mother's house and working as a maid right now, but she has a cousin in Glasgow so she'll be going there soon. She's a lovely young woman, in her early twenties, I'd say, but she's pretty useless as a maid. I don't think she's ever done housework before. Her husband is an accountant. He was sent to one of the camps. Goody is writing letters to try to get him out but he says the red tape is dreadful. Can you imagine? Your husband is taken away and then you have to move to a country where you can hardly speak the language just to survive?" My mother shook her head sadly, and the other women made sympathetic noises.

I knew the young woman my mother was talking about. Her name was Grete and I really liked her. I had met her only a few times, but she was always very nice to me. Once she gave me a windup toy of a peasant woman carrying a broom, her hair covered by a kerchief. When I turned the key in her back and put her down on a table, she scurried along, sweeping crumbs. She looked so real, she seemed magic. Grete told me that the best toys in the world were made in Germany.

"I spoke to Hetty Cohen last week," Betty Young said. "She offered to take one of the boys. She thought he'd be good company for her David, being around the same age. But he still wets the bed. Eleven years old and not toilet trained! Can you imagine?" The other women shook their heads in disbelief. "Foreigners just aren't like English people," Betty said with a sigh. "Hetty said he was really difficult too. Refused to eat and shut himself up in his room. So she brought him back here. Told them he was too hard to manage."

"I thought of asking for a girl," another woman said. "But they've only brought boys into this hostel. People say the boys are more of a priority." She lowered her voice to a whisper and leaned forward. "Because they're circumcised, they can't hide the fact that they're Jewish."

"Well, my older half-brother Victor has four boys of his own and he always wanted a daughter," my mother said. "He told the Kindertransport people he'd like a girl. They phoned when the children arrived and asked him to come and choose one, but he refused. He told them, 'Send me the girl nobody else wants.' So he got this enormously fat fourteen-year-old from Vienna. My sister-in-law, Blume, is putting her on a diet and making her exercise every morning."

This was the first time I'd heard that my uncle had taken in a refugee. I wondered how long she would stay and whether I would get to meet her. Uncle Victor and his family lived in the London suburb of Ilford, where he had a successful tailor and furrier business like my Uncle Goody. Because Victor was a son of my grandfather's second wife, though, he was much older than my grandmother's children —almost as old as my grandmother herself—and his children, my half-cousins, were closer in age to my mother and her siblings than to me. His children and Bubbe's children had all played together when they were little, but they didn't see one another as regularly now.

The women continued chatting and I went back to my book. When their mending chores were finished, Mrs. Gerhardt wheeled in a trolley with tea and cookies. Bourbon biscuits: my favorite. Then it was time to leave. Brenda's clothes were dry by then. As I dressed her, I noticed the words "Made in Germany" stamped on the back of her neck. I whispered in her ear, "I'll take care of you, Brenda dear. Don't worry about those nasty German people. I won't let them put you in a work camp."

Chapter 4
Preparing for War

By July 1939, it looked as if Britain's involvement in the war was imminent. A leaflet dropped through letterboxes informed us that everyone would receive a gas mask and gave instructions for covering all windows for "the black-out."

Daddy and I sat at the breakfast table a few mornings later finishing our cornflakes and drinking tea while he read aloud from the *Daily Telegraph* and Mummy went to the kitchen sink to wash the dishes. She took two enameled bowls, filled one with soapy water and the other with clean water for rinsing, washed, rinsed, then stacked the clean dishes on the wooden draining board.

"Look at this," my father said. "It says here that if war comes, the whole country will have to be blacked out from sunset to sunrise so nighttime German bombers won't be able to see the cities. Everyone will have to cover their windows with black material, and they say to paste gummed tape over the window panes so if glass is shattered people won't be injured. 'No chinks of light will be allowed,' it says. 'No see-through curtains, no car headlights.' People won't even be allowed to smoke cigarettes outside."

I wondered why the grownups seemed so worried. I rarely went out at night and found it hard to imagine Croydon in total darkness.

My father saw a perfect business opportunity for Walltones. "I'll bring in black wallpaper and paint," he said. "It's going to take time for people to make curtains. They can paste wallpaper over the windows in a few minutes or they can paint the windows black."

He left early for the shop, where he phoned local suppliers, only to discover that other wallpaper retailers had come up with the same idea and the wholesalers were sold out. At last, he found one who still had black paper in stock, but the warehouse was in Hertford, about 50 miles away. Their business was cash and carry only; they refused to deliver.

"I'll have to buy a car," Daddy said.

"Don't be ridiculous, Marcus," my mother said. "We can't possibly afford a car. And, anyway, the only people who are supposed to be driving cars are doctors and other people who need them for essential work. And petrol's probably going to be rationed. How will you be able to run it?"

"Tilly, you don't know what you're talking about," he said. "This is too good an opportunity to miss."

Because everyone knew petrol was going to be rationed, buying a cheap car was easy. The 1933 Ford Daddy bought cost him four pounds ten shillings—about $400 today. With petrol already in short supply, he decided to run it on kerosene purchased at the hardware store.

My mother and I watched as he bent down in front of the old Ford to crank it with a handle. When the car started, it gave him a vicious kick, made a series of popping explosions and emitted billows of evil-smelling black smoke from the exhaust pipe. The smoke enveloped the car, covering it with a film of black greasy residue.

"It looks dreadful, Marcus," my mother said. "You'll have to wash it."

"Don't be daft, Till," he said. "It's the dirt that's holding it together."

Passersby pointed and stared as he drove up the street, the filthy car backfiring, wreathed in thick clouds of black smoke.

While he was gone, Mummy and I went to the local primary school to pick up our government-issued gas masks. Cardboard boxes loaded with masks were piled on trestle tables in the school cafeteria, sorted according to size. Members of the Women's Voluntary Service wearing dark green uniforms handed them out. At one end of the table, huge boxes held red-and-blue-colored gas masks for children. They were labeled "Mickey Mouse masks" but they bore little resemblance to the squeaky cartoon character I loved.

There were also strange suits for babies. The bottom part was canvas and the top looked like a diving bell with a celluloid facepiece. Each suit had a clumsy pump on one side. One of the WVS members showed an anxious mum how to put her baby in the suit and use the pump, but the poor little thing wriggled and yelled, its muffled screams the soundtrack to our exit.

The gas mask carrying cases were flimsy cardboard boxes about the size of a woman's small purse. They had strings attached which adults threw over their shoulders and children slung across their chests so they didn't drag on the floor. The boxes were awkward and bumped into other people. We were supposed to carry them with us whenever we left the house.

When we got home, Mummy read the instructions printed inside the box lid and we practiced putting our masks on.

"It says you have to hold your breath and put your chin in first," she said. "Then it says to place the straps over your head and adjust them for a comfortable fit. Let's do it together."

I breathed in the strong smell of rubber mixed with disinfectant as we both followed the instructions.

"How does it feel?" she asked. It was difficult to understand her with the mask muffling her voice.

"It's hard to breathe in," I said.

"I suppose we'll get used to it," she replied.

We went to view our reflections in the mirror and thought we looked like a couple of Martians in a cartoon. I started to laugh but when I breathed out hard, the rubber around my face made a funny farting noise. As I laughed even more, the visor steamed up so it was difficult to see. Later, when we did gas mask drills in school, everyone in the class collapsed with laughter at the vulgar noises we made.

That night, my father returned triumphant from the wholesaler, the rattling old Ford packed with rolls of wallpaper and gummed tape, and cans of black paint.

The next day, he piled up the wallpaper and paint cans in the shop window and surrounded them with big rolls of tape. Walltones' window displays had always been showstoppers and this one was no exception. Customers shoved one another in the long line that formed outside the store, and he sold out in one day. The car had been a sound investment. He came home that evening with a big box of chocolates for us to share as a sort of celebration.

When I got home from school the next day, I watched my mother crisscross gummed tape over all our windows, using a sponge soaked in water to wet the tape and grumbling when water ran down her arms and dripped off her elbows. Then she stuck a roll of the black wallpaper onto the wall above the windows and, that night, she and my father unrolled it. When I walked to school the next day, nearly all the windows on our street had been taped like ours, making them look as if they were covered with trellises.

PART TWO:
WAITING AND WATCHING

Chapter 5
Leaving Home

I sat on the sheepskin rug, playing with our dog, Judy. My parents were listening to Prime Minister Neville Chamberlain's speech on the radio announcing Britain's declaration of war on Germany. That same evening, King George came on the radio and I sat up straight to listen. He spoke very, very slowly as he warned us of "dark days ahead" and told us, "War can no longer be confined to the battlefield." My parents looked worried.

The next morning, Mummy woke up with severe diarrhea, but when she ran to the pharmacy at the end of the road for a bottle of Kaopectate, the pharmacist said they were sold out. Everyone's stomach had turned to water at the thought of war.

Daddy went into Walltones and put a sign on the window: SALE. EVERYTHING MUST GO. In a few days he closed the shop and volunteered for the Auxiliary Fire Service. My parents knew fighting fires caused by the impending air raids would be dangerous, but serving in the Fire Service would be preferable to being conscripted into the army and shipped overseas.

My father reported for duty at the local fire station and immediately began a rigorous training program, shinnying up ladders and dragging heavy hoses. One day, he invited my mother and me to observe training exercises. We were supposed to cheer him on as he climbed up swaying extension ladders and leapt onto rooftops, but I closed my eyes and held my breath. It was all too scary to watch. .

My father sold the car after war was declared and rode his bicycle to and from the fire station. He came home one foggy evening after training and plopped down into an armchair. "Whew! It was dreadful riding home," he said. "Drivers aren't allowed to use their car headlights and all the street lights are out. A car nearly hit me, and when I got to our street I couldn't see where the road ended and the pavement began. I veered right off the road at one point. It's a good thing there were so few pedestrians. It's pitch-dark out there."

"I tried to buy a flashlight today," my mother said. "But Woolworths was all sold out. Becky Cowan told me she found one but she couldn't buy batteries anywhere."

Ever since I could remember, we'd had a live-in housekeeper. My Welsh Grandma Polly had interviewed miners' daughters in Merthyr and selected Betty, the oldest of seven children, to come to Croydon. Betty had started working for us when she was 14 and I was two and a half. She took care of me and did all the laundry, cooking and housework while my mother worked in the shop. But when war broke out and my father closed the shop, my parents could no longer afford such a luxury.

When my mother told Betty she would have to go back home to Wales, Betty burst into tears. "Please, Ma'am, don't send me back home. I love being hyur."

"I'm sorry, Betty," my mother said. "We just can't afford you anymore. I'd love to have you stay, but Mr. Shelower has joined the Fire Service and they don't pay enough for us to keep you."

"I'll work for you for nothing Ma'am'," Betty sobbed. "Don't send me back there. Me Da is dyin' of the black lung, and me sister has TB."

"Betty, dear," my mother replied. Her voice sounded wobbly, and her nose had grown very red. "We won't be able to afford the food for you."

The next day my mother and I walked with Betty to the station. All three of us cried when she got on the train.

Betty's chores now became my mother's. Mummy became a regular housewife, a role she didn't enjoy. She hated housework and wasn't very interested in cooking. She much preferred working outside the home and paying someone else to keep house. But now she had no choice.

Newspapers warned that the London area would be a prime target for Hitler's bombs. In anticipation, the government organized a huge evacuation program and, in the first four days of September 1939, nearly three million children were sent away from London and other target cities to stay in the countryside.

My parents believed that, as Jews, we would be singled out for Nazi persecution and that, as a Jewish child, I especially would be in danger if German soldiers landed on our shores. They decided I would be safer out of the country and put my name on a waiting list with one of the many orgaizations that had begun evacuating children to Canada and the United States.

"It'll be so exciting," my mother said when she told me about their decision. "You'll be sailing on an ocean liner. Just like going on a very big holiday."

I tried to feel excited but inside I felt dread. My parents and I had gone by ship on holiday to Belgium last August and I remembered the disgusting smell when we went below deck. Mummy had told me the smell came from something called bilge water and I should hold my nose. Would the ship to America or Canada smell like that? I hoped not. And who would I stay with when I reached my destination?

My parents heard nothing for weeks and I hoped they would forget about sending me away, but they didn't. Instead, rather than enroll me in the government's domestic evacuation program, which gave them no say in where I'd be sent, they decided it would be better for me to stay with family members who lived in a safe area. Mum wrote to Auntie Dolly, my father's sister, asking if I could come to stay with his family in Merthyr Tydfil.

I overheard my mother reading Dolly's reply aloud to my father.

"We could be bombed here in Merthyr, too," Auntie Dolly had written. "And, as you well know, my mother is very ill."

I thought Auntie Dolly didn't sound very welcoming. My parents, however, were determined I should go anyway.

"It won't be for long, dear," Mummy said. "I read an article in the paper this week saying the war will be over by Christmas."

I'd stayed overnight by myself at Bubbe's house many times, but I'd never been left alone in Merthyr. When I'd visited with my parents, we'd always been together. Now I was going to stay there by myself—perhaps for a long time.

We lived on the two top floors of a big Victorian house on a tree-lined street. My parents owned the house, and my father had converted it into two apartments so the downstairs tenants could provide them with extra income. My father took care of the large backyard, shaded by a huge beech tree, which scattered small nuts all over the lawn in the fall. On hot summer days, the tenants, skinny old Mrs.

James and her sad-eyed spinster daughter, Marjorie, would set up deck chairs outside their French doors and bask in the sunshine, but taking care of the garden was my father's responsibility. Every September, he climbed the gnarled apple tree and picked apples, placing them in a small bucket with a string attached to the handle. I waited below and tipped the apples gently into a laundry basket. Mummy had a light hand with pastry, and she baked pies with a melt-in-the-mouth crust. The rest of the apples were shared with friends and family.

I roamed around the apartment and the back garden, wondering how long I would be away and when I would see all the familiar things again.

My mother helped me pack for my stay in Merthyr. She'd taught me to read when I was four, so I chose *The Children's Omnibus*, a collection of stories and poems. It was a huge book and would add to the weight of my suitcase but I never got tired of the treasures inside.

"You can pick one toy to play with when you go," she said. Of course, I chose my doll Brenda and picked out two dresses for her.

Early the next morning, Mum and I set off on the long journey to Wales. Since we had to have our gas masks with us at all times, we slung the cardboard cases over our shoulders, but my string got tangled up with Brenda's sweater. I put her over my shoulder and Mummy carried the suitcase. We boarded the train from East Croydon Station to London Victoria and then caught a bus to Paddington Station, where we would board yet another train to Wales.

Paddington was filled with crowds of evacuee children traveling alone, escorted by only a few official chaperones. Luggage labels bearing their names and addresses were looped through coat buttonholes. Everyone had gas masks slung over their shoulders just like us and each child carried a bag or pillowcase holding their clothes and a paper bag containing food for the day. Many looked scared and some were crying. I tightened my grip on my mother's hand.

"You're a lucky girl," she said. "You won't have to stay with strangers." You'll be with Grandma Polly and Auntie Dolly and Nellie."

The train to Cardiff was so full of men in uniform there were no seats left, so we sat on our suitcases in the train corridor for the two-and-a-half-hour journey, passing through small towns and farmland outlined with hedges. From Cardiff, we took the local steam train, which huffed along, stopping at small mining towns along the way. The landscape was peppered with huge slag heaps of coal, the sky gray with rain and smog. Grimy miners entered our compartment, filling it with the smell of coal dust, and Mummy took out an embroidered handkerchief and held it daintily up to her nose.

Finally, we disembarked at Merthyr station and took a taxi to my grandparents' home, located on a road of gracious Victorian houses called The Walk. The house's name, Hazelmere, shone from a brass plaque attached to the gate. Too grand to have a street number, I thought.

As we entered the foyer, I was glad to see a cat and a couple of kittens scuttle into the kitchen at the back of the house. I'd been sad to leave Judy behind and hoped the cats would make the big house a little more welcoming.

Chapter 6
Merthyr Tydfil

My mother and I shared a bed that night, exhausted after our long journey. The next morning, we sat side-by-side on the bed and she put her arm around me. "I have to go back to London now, darling," she said.

"When can I come home?"

"Soon. Very soon," she said. Tears seemed to spurt out of her eyes, her delicate nose grew red and her eyelids swelled. I'd never seen my mother cry. My stomach lurched as I tasted my own salty tears. I threw my arms around her neck and clung to her, suddenly afraid.

"Don't go. Don't go," I cried.

She loosened my embrace and said, "I must, darling. I have to catch the train." Then she gave me a quick hug, kissed me goodbye and was gone.

I threw myself face down on the bed and sobbed. In a few minutes, Auntie Dolly came into the room.

"Now now, Cynthia. Stop that cryin'. Let's go wash your face." Her words had a Welsh sing-song lilt. She took me into the bathroom, stood me at the washbasin and dabbed my face with a wet washcloth. I glanced at her reflection behind mine in the mirror: a sharp, long nose like Daddy and Grandpa Barney; wavy black hair and sparkling brown eyes. I thought she looked a bit like a blackbird.

"Come on down now," she said. "It's breakfast time and I have to take Grandma her tray."

I could hear loud moans coming from the big front bedroom at the end of the hall. My grandmother Polly, riddled with cancer, was calling out "Mama. Mama." How could she ask for her mother? I thought. She was much too old to have a mother. She was 56.

Auntie Nellie came out of Grandma's room as I was heading downstairs. She gave me a big smile and a quick hug. "Cynthia! Look how big you're getting. I'm so happy you're here." She patted my cheek. "I'll see you later. I have to go to the shop now." I really liked my Auntie Nellie. She was cheerful and smart. I hoped we'd be able to spend more time together.

Downstairs in the dining room, after Auntie Dolly cleared away the breakfast dishes, Grandpa sat at the table with a new deck of cards in his hand. He folded back the flowered tablecloth to expose a green plush one underneath, opened the deck and sprinkled the cards with salt so they wouldn't stick together. Then he shuffled them like a magician, so fast they were like froth in his hands. Finally, he laid them out in seven columns for a game of solitaire. A cigarette drooped from his mouth beneath a beaky nose and nicotine-stained moustache. Dark blue eyes squinted behind the smoke clouds. Between rapid flips of the cards, he took the cigarette out of his mouth and slurped steaming hot tea from a big cup. I watched him, seated at the head of the table, skinny and bent, and marveled at the total hairlessness of his head, shiny as marble, mottled with blackened freckles and moles. Grandpa ignored me, mesmerized by the cards.

I sat beside the closed, coal-burning stove, watching Grandpa and stroking one of the kittens. Her soft fur was comforting in this strange house where Grandma lay upstairs crying like a baby, Grandpa didn't seem to know I was there, Auntie Nellie had disappeared out the door and Auntie Dolly, rattling dishes in the scullery, seemed too preoccupied to pay any attention to me. I thought longingly of my other grandmother's house, where my aunts, uncle, and Bubbe hung on my every word. This place was so different.

I soon grew bored watching Grandpa, put the kitten down, wandered down the hallway to the closed parlor door and reached up to pull down the door handle. Inside, the room smelled stale. On the floor was a bearskin rug, the bear's lips drawn back in a fierce grimace, snarling, his teeth pointed. His glass eyes stared at me and I drew back. He was so scary. A clock stood on the mantle covered by a glass dome. Golden gears twirled and clicked inside and a little pendulum swung gently back and forth. On the coffee table was a celluloid owl's head. The beak looked loose. What would happen if I pressed it? Timidly, I pushed it down and the head rang loudly like a bell. I turned it over and discovered a crank key, wound it and made the owl ring again. An upright piano stood against a wall. It was the first time I'd ever been in a house with a real piano. I put the clockwork owl down and spun around on the piano stool. I lifted the shiny black lid and pressed a few keys.

At the sound of the notes, Auntie Dolly came running in. "Don't do that, Cynthia," she snapped. "It bothers Grandma. Don't touch anything in hyuh. D'you understand?" Dolly seemed to have a really short temper. She didn't speak to me softly like my mother and her family did. I felt stinging behind my eyelids and looked down at the floor so she wouldn't see me cry.

Mummy had told me that when Dolly was younger, she had played piano extremely well and had such a beautiful voice that she'd taken singing lessons from a private teacher. She said Auntie Dolly had wanted to be an artist or musician but Grandpa said no and when Grandma Polly became ill he made her keep house and help in the shop. Maybe that was why she was grouchy and got so angry at me for touching the piano keys.

Dolly's wedding had taken place a few months earlier in Grandma's bedroom under a wedding canopy surrounded not by flowers and joyful guests but bedpans and the smell of disinfectant. She was back living with her parents because her husband, my new Uncle Sidney, a plump man who wore thick glasses, had volunteered for the army. Dolly was pregnant, separated from her new husband, taking care of her invalid mother, keeping house for her father, and now she had to take care of me.

Dinner that night was a stringy meat stew accompanied by stodgy noodle pudding and boiled potatoes that lay leaden in my stomach. For dessert, Dolly produced a dry layer cake with the texture of sand. The filling was blackcurrant jam made with blackcurrants from the garden and a kind of imitation butter cream made with margarine and gritty sugar because no confectioner's sugar was available. I wasn't able to swallow the tough blackcurrant skins, so I spat them out discreetly into my hand and put them on the side of my plate.

The next day was Sunday and I woke up early. Watery sunshine streamed in through the bedroom window. I lay on my back thinking of my usual weekend routine back in Croydon. I would have padded down to my parents' bed for a Sunday morning cuddle. Squeezed between them, we would make a "Cynthia sandwich." My eyes began to prickle as I stared at the ceiling and remembered.

Dolly interrupted my thoughts. "Get up and get yourself dressed, Cynthia," she said.

I struggled clumsily into my clothes. My mother always helped me get dressed in the morning.

"Cynthia, you haven't combed your hair," Auntie Dolly said at the breakfast table.

"Mummy always combs my hair and ties it with a ribbon," I said.

"Hmm. We'd better get you some barrettes," Dolly said. "A big girl like you should be able to comb her own hair."

"I'll find some pretty ones for her," Nellie said. "I'll be in the shop tomorrow and can drop into Woolworths on my lunch hour."

I spent the rest of the day playing with Brenda, reading and playing with the kitten.

After dinner that evening, we were sittiing around the table drinking tea when Auntie Nellie put down her glass and cleared her throat. "I have something to tell everyone," she said. "I applied for a factory job and I got a letter yesterday saying I've been accepted."

Dolly and Grandpa put their tea glasses down and stared at her. They didn't look happy.

"They haven't told me where I'll be working yet," Nellie continued. "The factory locations are secret. But I'll have to relocate, so I'll be moving out. I'm supposed to start in a week."

"Moving out?" Grandpa said. "Can't you work in a factory in Swansea and still stay home?"

"I guess they don't need people there. You have to go where you're needed."

"But how can a young girl like you move out of her parents' house?"

"I'm not a young girl anymore, Dad. I'm twenty-five. Anyway, it'll be one less mouth for you to feed, Dolly."

Dolly looked upset. "But we need you here, Nellie," she said. "How can I manage with mother so ill? Why didn't you ask Pa and me first?"

"I guess I knew you'd try to stop me, and I wanted to do my bit for the war effort."

"But what about us?" Dolly said. "What about your family?"

"I'm sorry," Nellie said. She got up from the table and left the room.

Grandpa and Dolly watched her go. Then Grandpa laid his playing cards out on the tablecloth to play solitaire and Dolly cleared away the tea glasses. Neither said another word.

I felt sad that Auntie Nellie was going to move out of Grandpa's house. She was the only person who was fun to be with.

Lokshen Kugl (**Noodle Pudding**)

- 1 pound vermicelli
- 1 teaspoon salt
- 2 eggs
- 4 ounces margarine
- 1 cup sugar mixed with 2 teaspoons cinnamon
- ½ cup white raisins

1. Add salt to 10 cups water and bring to a boil in a large pot.
2. Add vermicelli and boil according to package directions.
3. Drain in a colander. Run cold water over the vermicelli and drain again. Transfer to a large bowl.
4. Melt margarine in a saucepan and let cool slightly.
5. Beat eggs in a small bowl. Mix in melted, cooled margarine.
6. Add egg mixture to the vermicelli, tossing the noodles by hand.
7. Mix in sugar and cinnamon, then raisins.
8. Grease a 9" x 13" baking dish. Tip vermicelli mixture into the dish.
9. Bake at 350 degrees for 40-60 minutes or until noodles begin to brown.

Cynthia Ehrenkrantz

Chapter 7
New Gel

T he next morning, two neighbor children, Joan and
Sheila, stopped by and we walked together to the
local state school. I was assigned to Standard One,
where we were given paperback reading primers. Mine was
Puss in Boots, the words hyphenated into syllables. I finished
the story in a couple of minutes, then went to the teacher to
ask for another book.

She looked at me skeptically.

"Come come now, Cynthia. You can't have finished it
that quickly."

"Yes I have, Miss." I replied. "It's the story of Puss in
Boots and how he goes up to London to meet the mayor."

"Read it to me then," she said. After listening to me
gabble through the first couple of pages, she scribbled a
quick note and told me to take it to the teacher in Standard
Two.

When I arrived, the pupils were practicing penmanship,
laboriously copying sentences from the blackboard. The
teacher, Miss Owen, read the note I handed her and told me
where to sit. When the bell rang, she announced it was time
for arithmetic.

"Let's start with our five times," she commanded, then
began tapping a crisp rhythm on the desk with her ruler.

Whose five times? I thought. They certainly weren't
mine. An obedient chorus started to recite in a Welsh sing-
song: "One times five is five. Two times five is ten. Three
times five is fifteen...."

It sounded like a foreign language to me. At Coloma
Convent and Miss Cleal's we'd used bead frames for
counting. I had sneakily tried to pull my frame apart once

because I thought the beads would make a pretty necklace, but I'd succeeded only in bending the wires the beads were threaded on. Before I'd left, we had started learning our multiplication tables but had only got as far as the threes. "One three is three, two threes are six, three threes are nine...." One times five is five made no sense to me whatsoever. I slumped miserably in my seat trying to mouth the words but they could have been in Swahili.

At lunchtime, I ate the jam sandwich Dolly had made for me and went out to the playground. I looked in vain for Joan and Sheila because I needed to use the toilet and didn't know where it was. On one side of the school building was a rickety looking shed where I saw a door marked Girls. Inside was a splintery wooden board over a hole. And the smell! Yuck! I backed out, gagging. There must be some other place to go, I thought. But the bell was ringing for us to go back to class so I followed the other children into the classroom.

I didn't go to my seat but stood next to the teacher as she tried to bring order to the class. "Please, Miss Owen," I whispered, "I have to go to the toilet." But she took no notice of me as she tried to calm the children. "Please, Miss," I said, jiggling from one foot to the other. Then I could hold it no longer and I felt the warm trickle down my leg as a flood was unleashed.

I stood in my own warm puddle in front of the class. Titters from the children crescendoed into roars of laughter as they pointed and cried out, *"Ych a fi!"* (*"Achevee!"*)— Welsh for "Ugh! Disgusting!" I started to cry and was sent to the school office, where dry underpants were stored for accidents like this one.

Walking me back to Grandpa's after school, Joan and Sheila pretended they weren't with me. Children giggled and pointed at me all the way home, even from the other side of the road. From then on, I was known as "the gel from London who wet herself."

Grandma's health continued to deteriorate. Much as I hated school, I dreaded coming back each afternoon to the big sad house with the nasty smell even more. Nurses padded back and forth carrying covered bedpans, and people whispered instead of holding a normal conversation. Auntie Nellie left for her new job and Auntie Dolly was growing very fat and seemed to be tired all the time.

Grandpa mostly ignored me. He left for Papertones in the morning, came home briefly for lunch and went back to work until dinner. On Thursday evenings, a group of his cronies came to the house to play poker. Only then did he seem to liven up a little. Auntie Dolly served kichel to the crew: good for dipping in their whiskey. The room became thick with cigarette smoke and crackled with Yiddish conversation I didn't understand. I wondered if Grandpa even knew I was living in his house.

I grew accustomed to being ignored and spent my afternoons after school struggling to write letters to my parents. My mother wrote frequently and sent me copies of *Enid Blyton's Sunny Stories,* a weekly magazine for young children. Each copy included a puzzle or coloring competition and I painstakingly wrote out the answers to the word puzzles or colored in the pictures, being very careful to keep inside the lines. Auntie Dolly, the family artist, found pastels for me, and I passed the long winter afternoons drawing and decorating the pictures in coloring books.

Chapter 8
Chicken Farming

By early January 1940, Grandma Polly was close to death and Dolly wrote to Mum, begging her to take me home. My mother came to fetch me and we traveled back to Croydon together. Grandma died a few weeks later.

When I came home from Grandpa's house, Croydon looked different. The iron railings that had stood around our local parks and front gardens had all disappeared.

"What happened to them?" I asked my mother.

"They've gone to factories to be melted down and made into guns," she explained.

The park itself looked different, too. Though I could still see some neat flower beds and wandering paths from the street, most of the park had been turned into "allotments"—family garden plots where people could grow their own vegetables. Before the war, Britain had imported more than half of its food. As soon as war broke out, German U-boats began patrolling the Atlantic and North Sea, intent on destroying merchant ships carrying food and other critical supplies, while British merchant vessels had to be reassigned to transporting military hardware. The government knew the country had to make every effort to become as self-sufficient as possible. The Dig for Victory campaign had been launched in October 1939 with public service posters, short films and government pamphlets encouraging people to grow enough vegetables to feed their families. My Uncle Goody had never put his hands in the dirt before, but he threw himself into gardening, determined to keep my grandmother supplied with vegetables for the duration of the war.

Posters warning that "Walls Have Ears" and "Careless Talk Costs Lives" were pasted on billboards and railroad station walls, and hundreds of huge, partially hydrogen-filled blimps called barrage balloons floated above us in the sky. Croydon's airport and factories were prime enemy targets, and the balloons were designed to foil German dive bombers. The size of a large truck, they looked like giant silver sausages tethered to the ground with steel cables. German bombers would be forced to fly above them to avoid getting ensared in the cables, which would limit their accuracy and make them easier targets for anti-aircraft guns. If a bomber shot or ran into a balloon, the balloon would explode, taking the plane down.

My parents had made their own preparations for air raids. Daddy had put two buckets near our front door, one filled with sand and the other with water. A stirrup pump stood next to the water bucket. To work it, he had to lower one end of the hose into the bucket, put his foot on the stirrup and pump, aiming the stream of water at the fire. This was the homemade equipment he hoped would help him fight a fire if a bomb fell on our house.

Contrary to expectation, though, no bombs were dropped immediately on London. Germany was occupied with the invasion of Poland, and battles were being fought at sea. The air raids we'd prepared for didn't start and things were eerily quiet. Adults called those first months of 1940 The Phoney War and people hoped the whole thing might be a false alarm.

I went back to Miss Cleal's School, and we resumed our old routine of going to Bubbe's house on most weekends as we had done before the war. My father came with us when he wasn't on duty at the fire station.

Even in wartime, Bubbe's house was steamy and full of seductive cooking smells. Before the war, she would put together packages of cast-off clothes, tuck pound notes into the pockets and mail them to her family in Poland. In exchange, they sent strings of dried mushrooms, the base for her mushroom-barley soup. The mushrooms filled her kitchen with a smoky, woodsy aroma. But they stopped coming in early 1940, and no more letters came from her family. She complained that soup made with fresh mushrooms wasn't nearly as good, and she worried constantly about the lost communication with her father, brothers and sister.

I was sitting at our kitchen table in Croydon with my parents one March morning, enjoying my breakfast: a soft-boiled egg served in an egg cup with my name on it, accompanied by a slice of brown bread, buttered and cut into strips we called "soldiers." I loved dipping the strips into the egg yolk.

My mother was reading the *Daily Mail.*

"Oh, no. Now they're rationing meat," she said. "I thought it was bad enough rationing butter, sugar and eggs, not to mention milk. Now meat. I have a child to feed. How are we going to survive?"

"Well, the first thing we should do is register ourselves as vegetarians," my father said. "It says in the paper that vegetarians will be entitled to two eggs a week instead of one, and extra cheese and nuts when they become available. You can do a lot more with half a pound of cheese than you can with half a pound of meat."

My father had been a health-food enthusiast for a long time, believing a vegetarian diet was healthier. My parents went to Croydon Town Hall where they registered our family as vegetarians, swearing that we didn't eat fish, flesh or fowl and surrendering our rationing coupons for meat and bacon. Fish, however, had always been an important part of our diet and we continued to eat it. Fish wasn't rationed and it was a staple part of our food supply, although there were always long lines at the fishmongers.

My mother took charge of our ration books. Because we were now vegetarians, she only had to register with a grocer. Meat eaters had to register with a butcher, too. Store registration helped the Ministry of Food determine how much to send to each shopkeeper. Ration coupons were used for food purchases and torn out or canceled with a rubber stamp. The coupons were not used instead of money. People still had to pay for rationed foods but prices were controlled.

We all had National Identity Cards. My national identity number was XHAV 272/7, and Mummy told me to memorize it because she was putting the card in a safe place. She was afraid I'd lose mine if I kept it with me.

As we were entitled to only two eggs per person per week, my father decided we should keep chickens. The government encouraged this, along with keeping rabbits.

My parents, both raised in cities, had owned cats and dogs but knew nothing about chickens. My father sent away for books on poultry farming, subscribed to a poultry industry magazine and went to the public library to learn about raising hens. He spent his next leave from the Fire Service building a henhouse in our backyard with a run enclosed by chicken wire, dowels for the birds to perch on and pullout trays under a wire floor, so he could remove the droppings to use as fertilizer on our garden. Once the henhouse was complete, he brought home a dozen young Rhode Island Red pullets. They were all supposed to be hens, but one turned out to be a cockerel who woke the whole neighborhood every morning with his crowing.

Getting food for the hens was a challenge, since it was illegal to give animals any food fit for human consumption. My father discovered that a local bakery was discarding stale bread at the end of the day, so he went there regularly to pick some up. The bread was supposed to go to pig farms, but since we didn't eat pork he rationalized we were entitled to it too. He mixed the bread with table scraps and sawdust from a local lumberyard. The hens grew plump, pecking their way up and down the long chicken run, gobbling up insects and grubs as we waited for them to start laying.

It was my job to check their nesting boxes. One day, I found a hen sitting comfortably on the thick straw and pushed her off gently. She'd laid an egg, but it looked weirdly transparent and I could see its shadowy yolk. When I picked it up, it collapsed into a gooey mess in my hand. The egg had no shell, just the membrane that lines a normal eggshell. I ran into the house, slimy raw egg all over my hands and dripping down my dress, crying with disappointment.

My father knew from studying his poultry books that hens need to eat grit to aid their digestion and provide enough calcium to form eggshells. He had assumed the ground they pecked at was gritty enough, but obviously it wasn't. He bought supplies of crushed oyster shells from the pet store, and the problem was corrected. Soon, I was collecting brown eggs with wisps of feathers attached. We washed them carefully and they became a staple of our diet. One way Mummy prepared the eggs was by first hard-boiling them, then slicing them in half and serving them with a creamy mushroom sauce over rice: gray, white and yellow on the plate like an elegant fashion statement.

Sometimes she baked eggs in ramekins with tomatoes and cheddar cheese. I loved these dishes. Of course, she made loads of omelets and lots of scrambled eggs and often served egg dishes for dinner. Keeping hens improved our wartime diet enormously.

It was Mum's job to feed the chickens and refresh their drinking water. A bottle attached to the chicken wire enclosure and turned upside down replenished their bowl. I loved watching the hens take dainty sips, stretching their necks out and up at the sky so the water could trickle down their throats. When my mother approached the chicken run, all the hens would scurry toward her, cackling anxiously. She became fond of them, gave them names and made clucking noises as she filled their dish.

We learned new facts about eggs. An egg less than one day old won't boil properly; the white tends to blend with the yolk. If you hard-boil very fresh eggs, they don't peel properly, either, and you lose a lot of the egg white. If you feed hens cod liver oil to ward off vitamin D deficiency and rickets, your eggs will taste fishy.

In the spring, some hens refused to get off the nest and insisted on sitting on their eggs. My father looked up this behavior and learned they were turning broody—determined to sit on their eggs until they hatched. He decided we could use some extra chickens, so he built individual nesting boxes separate from the chicken run, where these expectant mother hens sat on their eggs for three weeks, taking brief breaks to peck at grubs and relieve themselves in their private runs. This gave me a chance to watch the eggs as I waited for them to hatch. One day, an egg started rocking back and forth of its own accord. I squatted down close to the nest and watched patiently until a tiny beak appeared and, after a lot of pecking at the egg from the inside, a slimy, bedraggled chick broke out of its shell, exhausted. The mother hen stroked its wet feathers with her beak until it turned into a little ball of yellow fluff.

The next time Mummy and I peeled hard-boiled eggs, she showed me how the membrane at one end of the egg was not attached to the shell. This little bubble provided air for the chick to breathe as he was pecking his way out of the shell. Such a perfect design, I thought. It was like a small miracle.

A few days after the chicks hatched, I was running in the backyard when I felt a sudden squelch under my foot just as a hen started cackling wildly. I'd accidentally stepped on a chick. I leapt back, horrified to see the squished intestines, still steaming, mixed with earth, yellow fluff and grass. I burst into tears and was very careful where I walked after that.

Eventually, egg production slowed. There was no point in feeding hens who weren't laying eggs, so my father decided to cull the flock and take a brief departure from vegetarianism. We followed kosher dietary laws, so my father couldn't just kill a chicken himself. For the meat to be kosher, the hen had to be killed by a *shochet*, a specially trained slaughterer who would make sure it was disease-free and kill it in the prescribed manner, draining it of blood. My father selected a plump nonlaying hen, tied her legs together with string and stuffed her into a zippered tote bag. My mother opened the zipper about half an inch so the hen's beak could poke through and we set off for a journey by train and bus to London's East End.

We had some difficulty finding the way from the bus station because there were no road signs. They had all been taken down after the Battle of Dunkirk when the possibility of a German invasion seemed like a real threat. If there were no roadsigns, Mummy explained, enemy spies and soldiers who dropped in by parachute or came ashore wouldn't know where they were. That was smart, I thought. Then they would have to ask for directions and their German accents would give them away.

On a side street, we finally came to a small slaughterhouse and heard alarmed cackling from chickens who seemed to be aware that their final moment was near. Our hen started wriggling in the bag and making little clucking noises as if she were trying to reply.

Inside the slaughterhouse, the noise of cackling and crowing was deafening. A stream of water mixed with blood flowed down a gutter in the floor and drained into one corner. We handed our hen over to a man who briefly inspected her and dipped her head and neck into a water bath. Then he passed her on to the shochet—a man with a scraggly beard who wore a blood-stained apron and held a long knife. He drew his thumb along the blade, muttered a little prayer and, in one swift movement, slit the chicken's throat. Then he turned her upside down and dumped her into a hole in a board, balanced on trestles. She twitched a couple of times and then flopped over, lifeless. He waited until her blood stopped dripping onto the floor, then handed her to a second man in an apron who reached in and pulled out her insides. Then this man handed her over to an old woman who sat outside the slaughterhouse, plucking the birds by hand. She wasn't very thorough, though, and our hen was left with lots of big spiny feathers all over her body. When we got home, Mummy spent over an hour in the kitchen finishing the job.

Eggs in Mushroom Sauce

- 3 cups cooked rice
- 8 hard-boiled eggs, peeled
- 1 medium onion, diced
- ½ pound mushrooms, sliced
- 1 tablespoon butter or margarine
- 2 cups milk
- 2 tablespoons flour
- Salt and pepper

1. Slice eggs in half. Set aside.
2. Sauté diced onion in butter over medium heat until translucent.
3. Add the mushrooms.
4. Turn heat to low and cover the pan. Simmer for 5-10 minutes until the mushrooms release their juices.
5. Uncover the pan. Add flour and stir for 2 minutes.
6. Keeping heat on low, slowly add milk and cook, stirring constantly with a wire whisk until sauce thickens.
7. Spoon rice onto plates. Spoon mushroom sauce over rice. Place sliced eggs on top.

Cynthia Ehrenkrantz

Chapter 9
An Uninvited Guest

On a late afternoon in July 1940, the doorbell rang. Answering the front door was my chore. This saved my mother from running up and down the steep stairs from our apartment on the top two floors. Grandpa Barney from Wales stood on the doorstep, carrying a large suitcase in one hand and a carryall in the other. Although it was a warm day, he wore a long black overcoat and Homburg hat like Winston Churchill's. The smell of stale tobacco wafted from his clothes and bedraggled moustache. When he bent down to kiss me, I shrank backwards and almost tripped on the step. He followed me upstairs to the kitchen where my mother was standing at the table, cutting up cauliflower.

"It's Grandpa, Mummy," I announced.

My mother wiped her hand on her apron and held it out.

"Well, this is a surprise. Nice to see you," she said, her voice sounding strangely hoarse. "Cynthia. Take Grandpa's hat and coat."

Grandpa put his suitcase down and sat at the kitchen table.

"I can't live mit dat gel," he said. "It's a terrible t'ing ven a fadder and a daughter don't get along. Ever since February ven Mama died, she's been a terrible person. Und so I've decided dat I vould like to come and live mit mein son."

My mother sat down heavily on the chair opposite him.

"Live with us?" she asked. Her face had turned a funny yellowish color. "I'll go upstairs and get a bedroom ready. You stay here Cynthia and keep Grandpa company."

Sitting opposite him, I didn't know what to say. I watched him pull out a pack of Player's Navy Cut cigarettes decorated with a picture of a bearded sailor, and a big box of Swan Vestas matches. He lit a cigarette and the smoke swirled up to the ceiling. As usual, he paid no attention to me. I buried my head in my collection of Hans Christian Andersen's stories, getting lost in the tale of the emperor and the nightingale.

When I'd stayed at his house, Grandpa had mostly ignored me. This was the first time I ever remembered him coming to visit us. I wondered if he'd be more interested in me here, in my own house. But he had already spread a deck of cards out on the kitchen table and was playing solitaire.

Soon, my mother came downstairs. "You're in the room next to Cynthia," she said. "Do you need help with your suitcase?"

"Nah, nah. I don't vant to be no trouble. It'll be good to be mit mein son."

He went upstairs to unpack and my mother went back to preparing dinner. Her face looked grim, her eyes unusually bright.

After a while, Grandpa came downstairs with the carryall, opened the zipper and brought out a metal teapot, a porcelain cup and saucer, a tea caddy filled with tea, a tea cozy, a can of condensed milk and a thin, round asbestos mat, just big enough to sit atop a stovetop burner, on which were printed the words "Fireproof. For better cooking. Your pot will not burn or boil over. Saves pans and fuel."

"Dis is how I like mein tea," he said. "It must be very hot, zo, after it's made, you put de pot on de mat mit a small flame underdenee. I only drink mein tea from de china cop. From dis cop tastes better de tea. De condensed milk is better fon fresh. Fresh milk makes cold de tea."

My mother's eyes grew very wide. She pursed her lips and breathed loudly through her nose.

When Daddy came home from the fire station, he was surprised to see his father seated in the best armchair, blowing clouds of cigarette smoke. They hugged and sat chatting in the dining room while my mother prepared the meal: cauliflower in cheddar cheese sauce with broiled tomatoes.

While we ate, Grandpa explained again why he'd come to stay with us. After Nellie left home and Grandma Polly died, it was just Grandpa and Aunt Dolly in the house with Aunt Dolly's new baby girl, Sylvia.

"Since mudder died, Dolly doesn't speak," Grandpa said. "She cries all de time and jost sits. She hired a nurse for de baby. Doesn't even take care of her herself. All she does is sit around crying. She vas alvays a terrible cook but, now, if she cooks anyt'ing it's burnt and I can't eat it. I fill up on bread mit margarine." Clearly he hoped things would be better in our house.

My mother listened without comment. But while she washed the dishes, she banged them so hard on the draining board I thought they might break.

It didn't seem to matter to Grandpa that Dolly was now a widow. Her husband, Sidney, had died in an army training accident while she was still pregnant. His commanding officer had been showing the men how to clean a gun, when it went off, killing my uncle instantly. A young widow with a new baby, mourning her husband and mother—it was no wonder she was depressed. The Merthyr house was big, drafty and hard to run, and Grandpa was bad-tempered most of the time. I remembered the way he had grunted at Dolly, shouting commands without a "please" or "thank you."

My mother sympathized with Dolly. She had never liked Grandpa, a grouchy, chain-smoking, compulsive gambler who barked orders at his wife and daughters like a drill sergeant. She had seen my father yell orders at his sisters when they were courting and was familiar with the adage "The apple doesn't fall far from the tree." But she'd paid no mind, determined that she would never let her Marcus become like his dad.

After dinner, my parents went into the kitchen and closed the door. They tried to keep their voices low, but I heard my mother explode into an angry tirade.

"How am I supposed to feed him when we're having trouble finding enough food for the three of us? How dare he tell me how to make tea. If he thinks he's going to order me about like Dolly, he's got another think coming."

"Come on now, Till," Daddy said. "He's an old man and he needs a place to stay. It's too much for Dolly. Don't you think we can manage to take him in?"

My mother sighed. "He did give me his ration book," she said, "so it will bring a little more food into the house. I suppose we can try it for a couple of weeks and see how things work out. You should ask him to pay us something, too." I heard no more arguing. Still, when she came out of the kitchen, Mummy looked really cross. I crept upstairs to get ready for bed all by myself, knowing I should stay out of her way.

My father's relationship with Grandpa had never been good. My mother told me that before she and Daddy were married, he had managed the Merthyr wallpaper store, and he and Grandpa had argued constantly about how the shop should be run. My father wanted to spruce it up and carry a better grade of merchandise while Grandpa insisted he knew what the miners could afford and what would sell. In Grandpa's eyes, his son was a terrible spendthrift, wanting to take a far bigger income out of the business than it could bear. Grandpa was also always irritated by my father's habitual lateness and lack of organization. He was constantly telling his son to write things down so he wouldn't forget them.

"Buy yourself a little book for a penny," he'd say. But the more he spluttered and complained, the more stubborn my father became and the more they fought.

The prospect of having Grandpa under his roof probably didn't fill my father with delight, either. But he was older now, a husband and father himself, and maybe he thought having Grandpa stay with us would provide an opportunity to repair old hurts and start afresh. While Grandpa was with us, Daddy sat chatting with him whenever he was home from the fire station.

Having Grandpa in the house caused extra work for my mother. Laundry was an exhausting job. A gas-fired copper boiler stood in the corner of the kitchen. Every Monday, Mummy filled it with water, using a hose attached to the kitchen faucet. While the boiler heated, she scrubbed at stains on a washboard propped up in the sink. When water in the boiler was really hot, Mum added soap flakes, put in all the white clothes and sheets and stirred them with a long thick stick. Colored clothes were washed in the kitchen sink. Rinsing out the soap was a huge task; then everything had to be put through a hand-cranked clothes wringer, excess water going into a galvanized tub on the floor. If weather permitted, my mother carried heavy baskets of wet laundry down to the backyard and pinned them to a clothesline. When it rained, clothes were hung indoors on wooden drying racks called clothes horses placed around the fire. Grandpa's long johns, sheets and shirts added to the pile, and my mother tut-tutted and sighed as she scrubbed the extra clothes. Grandpa never offered to help with anything;

he sat around, smoked, read the paper and played solitaire. My mother had always been short-tempered on washday, and my father and I knew we had to stay out of her way. Now she looked angrier than ever, snapped at me whenever I asked a question and frowned all the time.

My mother had never enjoyed cooking, so having an extra mouth to feed seemed like an intolerable burden. Although she ate with gusto, Mum regarded food preparation as a tiresome chore. Hours spent over the stove watching pot roasts or simmering soups were associated with her Polish, Yiddish-speaking mother. Now that we were vegetarians, she complained that cooking vegetarian food dirtied lots of utensils because she had to beat the eggs, grate the cheese and slow-simmer the beans. Meat and two vegetables left her with much less cleanup, she said. Mum had also always striven to be accepted as a Proper English Lady and had adopted many British food prejudices along the way. She regarded herbs and spices with deep suspicion. Food in our house had always been bland and frugal, with portions spooned onto our plates in small amounts. If my father or I dared to request a second helping, we were told, "There's enough there for another meal, y'know." I learned early that if I wanted a second helping of anything, I had to get it in the kitchen when dishes were piled up to be washed. Only then could I surreptitiously pull a leftover slice of potato out of the roaster and enjoy crunching the crisp edges stuck to the pan.

Instead of chatting about our day's activities during meals, as we had done before Grandpa came, we now ate in silence, and I watched my mother wince when Grandpa smacked his lips, slurped his tea and wiped his plate clean with a piece of bread. Table manners were important to her; she had taught me to take small bites, dab my lips daintily with a napkin and place my knife and fork neatly together at the end of a meal. Grandpa paid no attention to such niceties. He ate his food and never thanked my mother for anything. He was as grumpy as ever. He shushed me when I laughed loudly. I hated having to kiss him goodnight. His moustache was scratchy and it smelled.

One day, when he'd been with us for about three weeks, Grandpa said to Mummy, "You know vat I really like? Onions mit eggs. Dis is a good supper. Perhaps vun day you'll make?"

My mother had an especially strong aversion to onions. She hated the smell of them on her hands or on people's breath. My father, on the other hand, loved them. When he ate them and tried to kiss her, she would wrinkle her nose and say, "Ugh. You smell of onions," turning her face away in disgust.

Fortunately for my mother, onions were now in short supply. Before the war, men from Brittany had crossed the channel and ridden bicycles festooned with strings of onions all around town. They knocked on doors and there was no need for them to speak English. We always had one of those onion strings hanging in our kitchen. After Germany occupied France, Britain's supply of onions was cut off, so my mother had good reason to hold onto the ones she had left. But my father and grandfather both loved onions, and eggs were plentiful in our house because of our backyard chickens, so eggs and onions was an easy, cheap supper.

The next day, my mother chopped three large onions, heated a big cast iron frying pan and tossed them in oil until they were golden. She seasoned them liberally with pepper and salt, beat six eggs and stirred them into the pan. Our dinner was a pile of fried onions flecked with scrambled egg, and whole wheat bread spread with margarine. Daddy,

Grandpa and I enjoyed our supper immensely. Mummy ate plain scrambled eggs.

The day after that, while Grandpa sat at the dining table smoking and shuffling cards, the small room began to fill with the unmistakable ripe aroma of an old man breaking wind. The stench quickly became overwhelming. When my father came home from the fire station, my mother beckoned him into the kitchen, her lips rimmed white with anger.

"Your father is disgusting," she said with a shudder. "He has to leave. I can't stand it. I'm going to tell him he has to go back to Merthyr, to his own house."

Daddy pleaded with her to let Grandpa stay. If he repaired the relationship with his father, perhaps the old man would remember them kindly in his will, he reminded my mother. But if they sent him back to Merthyr, my father was sure he would be cut off from any inheritance.

My mother was not swayed. The next morning, she confronted her father-in-law.

"I'm sorry," she said. "It's much too difficult having you here when there's a war on. I have to ask you to go back to Wales."

"T'ank you for telling me dis," Grandpa said. "Iz besser zat ve be honest mit vun anodder."

The next day, Grandpa packed his bags and left.

Daddy was furious with Mum for sending his father away. Grandpa's visit and his banishment from our house made the poor relationship between father and son even worse. They had communicated only when necessary before Grandpa came to live with us and fell back into the same pattern when he returned to Merthyr.

Cynthia Ehrenkrantz

Chapter 10
The First Air Raid

Everyone knew that Croydon Aerodrome would be a prime target for German bombers. Even so, the first attack, on August 15, 1940, an event now known as Black Saturday, came as a surprise.

I got ready for bed after supper that evening and Daddy came upstairs to tuck me in. This was a real treat because he spent most nights at the fire station, but tonight he was on leave. He sat on the side of my bed and held my small hand in his big one. I loved the rough feel of the skin on his palms, work-worn from heaving heavy fire hoses.

"Let's say the *Sh'ma*," he said. And, as was our nightly ritual, we recited the Hebrew prayer together: "*Sh'ma Yisroel, Adonoi eloheynu, Adonoi echod.*" *Hear O Israel. The Lord is our God, the Lord is One.* Daddy plumped up my pillow so it felt like a nest around my head, then gave me a bristly kiss. "Goodnight, honeybunch," he said. I listened to the sound of his footsteps going down the stairs. Judy lay beside my bed on the cool linoleum.

Though it was only seven o'clock and still bright outside, my room was dark because my father had drawn the blackout curtains. I turned on the lamp on the wicker table next to my bed. Before the war, Auntie Rose had taken a cruise to Morocco and the ship had stopped at the island of Madeira, where she'd bought wicker nursery furniture for my room. I'd propped Brenda up on the small chair next to the child-sized-table with a cup and saucer in front of her from the Snow White tea set Auntie Fan had given me for my seventh birthday four months before. Brenda and I had enjoyed a tea party that afternoon. The rest of the tea set sat on top of the bookcase. Each cup, saucer and plate was decorated with a character from the Disney animated film.

I got up and put Brenda in her pram, covering her with a pink blanket that had been mine when I was a baby.

Back in my bed, I couldn't fall asleep so I pulled my copy of *Worzel Gummidge,* the story of a scarecrow who comes to life, out from under my pillow. I was just starting to read when the air-raid siren went off. We'd had warning drills regularly since the war began. The swooping wail of one factory siren would start a chorus as it was joined by all the sirens in town, making a roller coaster of deafening sound. It was so loud, I stuffed my fingers into my ears until the wailing notes faded away. I hated loud noises so much that, until I was six, I cried uncontrollably when balloons burst with a bang at birthday parties and had to be taken home.

When the wail died down, I went back to my book, waiting for the usual all-clear, the sound of one sweet sustained note that always went off a few minutes after the warning. But this time there was no all-clear.

Suddenly, my parents rushed in. "Get up, Cynthia," my father said, calmly. "Put on your dressing gown and slippers and bring your gas mask. This is a *real* air raid."

I pulled my bathrobe out of the wardrobe, grabbed my cardboard gas mask case, threw the string over my shoulder and followed my parents.

"Hurry up, Cynthia. We're going to the closet under the stairs," Mummy said, her voice quivering.

When we reached the first landing, I stopped. "I forgot Brenda!"

"No time for that," Daddy said. "We have to get into the shelter." I could hear Judy's nails clicking on the stairs behind us as we ran down.

Government pamphlets had advised that the safest place in a house to take shelter during an air raid was the ground-floor closet under the stairs. Before the war, ours had stored suitcases and steamer trunks. My parents had moved those up to the attic and now the space held a blowup mattress, a couple of old blankets and two folding chairs. A cardboard box in one corner held a large flashlight, a box of candles, matches, tin plates and cups, some cans of food and a can opener. A bucket filled with water stood next to it. A dim light bulb switched on when you pulled a string. The closet was the only room in our house that didn't have a mezuzah nailed to the doorpost—a small case containing a piece of parchment inscribed with the sh'ma prayer. The little room had a damp, stale smell and I held my nose as we entered.

Daddy blew up the mattress. I lay down on it and Mummy covered me with a scratchy blanket. Judy lay down beside me and licked my hand. My parents unfolded the chairs and sat down.

"Let's sing 'Ten Green Bottles,'" Mummy said. When we got to *seven green bottles a-hanging on the wall*, there was a roaring noise of planes in the distance that grew louder and louder. When we got to *five green bottles*, the deafening noise was directly overhead. Our voices trailed away and I put my hands over my ears.

Then there was an eerie, whistling sound followed by loud, earsplitting bangs and thuds. The floor shook under us and Judy started to whimper. I screwed my eyes shut so tight I could see little colored lights behind my eyelids. My stomach turned over and over and I felt as if I would throw up and have diarrhea all at the same time. I panted little short breaths – just like Judy did when she'd been running.

My father always carried a book in his pocket; he sat on his chair, flipping the pages but not reading. My mother knelt beside me, stroking my hair. "It's all right, darling," she said. Then she lay on the splintery floor next to the mattress and put her arms around me.

Daddy stood up. "They're bombing the aerodrome," he said. "I'm going up to watch the fireworks."

"Please stay with us, Marcus," Mum pleaded. "Let's stay together." But he left saying, "Back soon, Tilly." I could hear him running up the stairs, two at a time, to our parlor floor. Mummy looked cross and breathed hard through her nose. I buried my face in Judy's silky fur.

The thumps and bangs were farther away now. At last, they stopped and the all-clear sang out: one sweet note from all the factory sirens. Mum pulled out a cigarette and put it in her mouth, unlit. When she spoke, it dangled from her lower lip. "Let's go upstairs," she said.

I jumped up from the mattress, pushed the closet door open, ran up to my room, picked Brenda up and hugged her. "I'm so sorry I left you behind, Brenda," I said. "I'll never leave you alone again." As I was leaving the room, I kicked something: a cup from the tea set had fallen off the bookcase and broken.

I carried Brenda down to the kitchen, where my parents sat at the table, waiting for the kettle to boil for tea. I told them about the broken cup.

"It must have toppled off the shelf from the vibrations," Daddy said. "Don't worry, honey. I'll glue it back together for you."

We sat drinking tea while my father told us about the raid he'd watched from the living room window.

"I saw a real dogfight," he said. "The searchlights picked out a German plane and one of ours sprayed him with bullets till he spiraled to the ground." Daddy made circles in the air with his finger.

We all went back to bed but it was hard to fall asleep so I read *Worzel Gummidge* all the way to the end.

The attack was front-page news in the paper the next morning. "'German dive-bombers swooped on Croydon Aerodrome last evening in the first bombing raid in the London area,'" my mother read aloud to us at breakfast. "'Thirty Heinkel twin engine bombers escorted by Messerschmitt fighters came over and divided into two sections to attack.'" One bomb had hit an aerodrome building, and at least one plane had swooped down and machine-gunned people in the streets. "It says sixty people were killed and more were injured and taken to hospital," my mother continued. "Windows were blown out of houses and people on a bus were hit with flying glass, but otherwise there was not much damage in the town." The attack had been met by "terrific anti-aircraft gun barrage," she said, "and our fighters went up to intercept them. It says at least three German fighter planes were brought down over and around Croydon and our RAF pilots destroyed others on their way back to Germany."

As Mummy held the newspaper up, I could see a photograph on the front page of the wreck of a German airplane. A badly damaged house was behind it and I wondered what had happened to the people inside.

After breakfast, Daddy fastened the metal buttons on his fireman's jacket and got ready to leave. "I'm going to get one of those Anderson shelters and put it up in the backyard," he said. "It looks as if the war is finally starting."

Cynthia Ehrenkrantz

Chapter 11
The Blitz Begins

T he August 15 bombing of Croydon was followed by another the very next day in nearby Merton and six more in the Croydon area before the month of August was out. Other cities and towns near bases, docks and factories also came under frequent attack. British forces retaliated by bombing Berlin, which so enraged Adolph Hitler that he ordered the Lufwaffe to switch from bombing British military and industrial sites to targeting London and other urban areas. The bombing began on September 7, 1940. It lasted eight months and was known as the Blitz.

The weekend after Black Saturday, I helped my father install the Anderson shelter in our backyard. Named for Sir John Anderson, the Home Secretary and Minister of Home Security, these shelters were supposed to save lives. Even in closets under the stairs, people didn't stand much chance of survival if their house got a direct hit. Anderson shelters were distributed free to people who earned less than 250 pounds a year—about $20,000 today; and since my father's weekly pay was three pounds ten shillings, about $275, we qualified easily.

The shelter was made of corrugated steel sheets that had to be bolted together at their curved tops, and my job was to sort the nuts and bolts my father had set out on a tarpaulin sheet on the lawn. He dug a pit three feet deep and sank the straight ends of the steel sheets into the ground so the walls were firmly embedded in the soil and the finished structure would be half below ground. Next, he bolted the curved top ends together to form a roof and attached the front and back sheets. Then he covered the entire structure with about a foot of earth and put sandbags on the roof and around the outside. My parents moved our canned food, flashlights and candles from the closet under the stairs into the Anderson and set up four army cots to accommodate my mother and me, and our tenants, Mrs. James and Marjorie. My father slept at the fire station when he was on duty. When he was on leave, I shared my mother's cot. The shelter was cramped and left little room for moving around. Bunk beds would have been better, but Daddy was too busy to build them. My father was over six feet tall and couldn't stand upright inside the shelter.

From then on, we retreated to the Anderson whenever the air-raid siren sounded and remained there until the all-clear.

On September 7, 1940, air-raid sirens wailed as soon as it was dark.

"Put your coat on," my mother said. "It's cold outside." I threw a scratchy woolen coat over my pajamas and Mummy and I padded through the wet grass. Barrage balloons glistened overhead and searchlights crisscrossed the sky, lighting our way as we stumbled across the backyard to settle into the Anderson.

Mrs. James and Marjorie were already there. We weren't supposed to bring dogs into shelters, so Mummy and I had left Judy in the house, but our shelter-mates had brought Bozo, their smelly fox terrier.

I found it hard to fall asleep in the dank cold. The shelter smelled so bad. Bozo farted a lot and Mrs. James had an odd, unwashed old lady smell. I pulled the heavy army blanket over my head, trying to shut out sounds of heavy breathing and snores, and was just starting to doze off when I was startled awake by Mrs. James turning on her flashlight. Its thin beam illuminated the inside of the shelter making creepy shadows on the walls. She was sitting bolt upright with her hand cupped to her ear.

"Hark! Hark!" she said. "Shh! Listen. I think it's one of ours." We all heard the drone of planes in the distance.

"Turn that light off," my mother commanded. "You're wasting the battery and it might shine out through the doorway."

As the plane's roar grew louder, Mrs. James started moaning and making desperate-sounding little gasps. "Oh, no," she said. "It's one of theirs."

"Do be quiet, Mrs. James," my mother said. "You're frightening the child." And, indeed, I was shivering as much from fear as from the cold.

Mrs. James was right. It was one of theirs. We heard a whistling screech and then a huge explosion. The ground trembled and our little refuge rattled. A bomb had landed really close to us.

Mrs. James screamed, "Oh my God! Oh my God! Sweet Jesus save us! We're all going to die!" I stuffed my fingers in my ears.

Gradually, the roar of airplanes faded away. Mrs. James lay down and we all tried to go to sleep, but by now I was wide awake and bone-cold. My blanket had got all tangled up and I couldn't fix it. I tried to find my flashlight, but it must have rolled away. I wanted to touch the warmth of my mother's body, to nestle into her soft belly and feel the tightness of her arms around me. I groped around in the blackness, feeling my way across the damp earth floor, weaving around the cots and tripping over the panting dog, who growled. At last I felt a warm reclining figure. Certain it was my mother, I reached out to gently touch her face. My hand sank into something slippery, slimy and wet: Mrs. James's mouth sans her false teeth.

"Drat dat child!" Mrs. James yelled. "Get opp me! Get opp!"

"I'm over here, darling," my mother said. I followed the sound of her voice, fell into her welcoming arms and settled into an uneasy sleep.

In the morning, when my father came home, he told us the bomb had fallen less than a mile away, on Lower Addiscombe Road. Three houses had been demolished, and all the people living inside had been killed.

When my mother and I walked up the street the next morning, smoke and dust hung in the air, making us cough. The bombed building was a heap of rubble, and broken glass littered the street from windows blown out by the blast. But as we got further into town, shopkeepers were opening their shutters and arranging their merchandise, determined to conduct business as usual.

Nightly bombing in the autumn of 1940 was relentless. Each time the air-raid sirens wailed, I felt ready to throw up. The back of my neck prickled and my clenched hands grew clammy. Nights of sleeplessness in the smelly Anderson shelter made us all edgy. I caught a bad cold that wouldn't go away.

One day, I overheard my parents speaking in low tones when they thought I was out of earshot: "...get her away... disturbed sleep .... safer somewhere else...."

My parents had all but forgotten they'd put me on a waiting list for overseas evacuation until two tragic incidents reminded them of it. The onset of the Blitz had triggered a second, two-pronged government-organized evacuation of children—some to safer parts of the country, others overseas to Commonwealth countries and the U.S. The evacuation ships traveled in convoys, but that did not always keep them safe. On August 30, 1940, a German U-Boat attacked the *SS*

Volendam bound for Canada with 320 children aboard. Fortunately, everyone survived except for one crew member. Eighteen days later, on September 17, a U-Boat attacked another evacuation ship, the *SS City of Benares*, bound for Canada with 90 children on board. This time, 293 people including 83 evacuee children died.

Overseas evacuation was now no longer an option because the program had been terminated after this tragedy. My parents decided instead that my mother and I should move to a safer area somewhere in the countryside. My father would stay behind, spending his nights on duty with the Fire Service, putting out fires from incendiary bombs and high explosives. Rural counties in the south of England seemed to be quiet, so they looked for a place close enough for my father to come and stay when he was on leave. My parents' friends, the Sabel family, had already moved to the little farming village of South Godstone, about 15 miles south of Croydon. The upper floor of a house on their street was available. My parents decided Mummy and I should move there. My mother packed our suitcases and we prepared to leave.

Cynthia Ehrenkrantz

Family Photos

My mother, Tilly Fox, Aged 20 (1926)

My father, Max Shelower, Aged 25 (1932)

My parents, Tilly and Max Shelower at their wedding.
(March 28, 1932)

Newborn me with my proud Daddy in the backyard of
Walltones, my parents' paint and wallpaper shop, before
clothes dryers were invented. (1933)

Howard M. King,   Croydon.

6 month old me with my mother, Tilly Shelower.(October 1933)

My Bubbe and nine-month-old me in the doorway of her
Palmers Green house.. (December, 1933)

I loved dressing up, even when I was 21 months old, in the backyard of the Croydon house my parents bought after they moved out of the apartment above their shop. (1934)

Cynthia Ehrenkrantz

2 year old me in the backyard of my Bubbe's house (1935)

My mother and 3-year-old me looking out of the window of my Bubbe's house. Auntie Rose is behind us. (1936)

6-year-old me vacationing on the beach in Ostend, Belgium. in August 1939, one month before Britain declared war on Germany

My parents holding hands at a family wedding. (1940)

My mother and her siblings with my grandmother
at a family wedding.
Front row: Half sister, Betsy Simons, sister Fanny Fox, my
grandmother, Rivke Fox, sister, Milly Betts.
Back row: Half brother, Victor Fox, sister, Rose Fox, my mother,
Tilly Shelower, brother Goody Fox
(1940)

My National Identity Card cover.

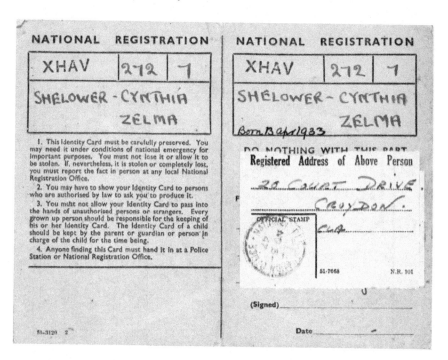

My National Identity Card interior.

My Grandfather from Wales. Berl (Barney) Shelower. (c. 1932)

DEAR CYNTHIA DARLING,
        I WOULD LIKE TO
HAVE A LETTER FROM YOU.
CAN YOU MANAGE TO WRITE
ME ONE. HOW ARE YOU
GETTING ON AT SCHOOL. DID YOU
GET THE FAIRY LAND TALES I
SENT YOU? AND THE WELLINGTON
BOOTS. AND HAVE YOU DONE
ANY MORE JOINED UP WRITING.
WE ALL SEND OUR LOVE, AND
BOOBA SENDS YOU A BIG KISS.
HAVE YOU BEEN TO SEE MRS
ROBOTTOM AGAIN. LOTS AND
LOTS OF LOVE TO YOU DEAR,
        FROM YOUR MUMMY.

One of the many letters my mother wrote to 6-year-old me when I was evacuated to Merthyr Tydfil. (1939)

Uncle Goody enjoying vacation, in France photographed by his nephew, Harry Fox. (1949)

Uncle Goody standing in front of his
Palmers Green shop. "Francine.
Dressmaker" was my Aunt Fan who
plied her needle upstairs.   (1937)

Labels like this one were sewn into every garment produced in
Uncle Goody's shop.

My father in his fireman's uniform.
(1942)

The house in South Godstone where my mother and I lived from 1940-1942. The weedy front yard I remember is now paved over to be used for parking.

This painting by a Croydon High School student depicts the scene my mother and I encountered when we entered the school after we were caught in a V-1 rocket air raid. in 1944

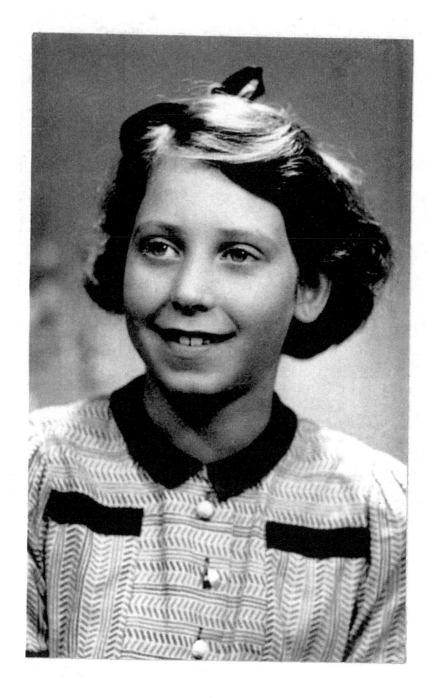

11-year-old me. (1944)

Grown up me standing in the field at the end of Rushton Avenue, in South Godstone, where my mother and I gleaned wheat for our chickens years earlier.

Cynthia Ehrenkrantz

PART THREE:
EVACUATION

Chapter 12
A New Normal

My mother and I arrived in the village of South Godstone at the beginning of October 1940. We were renting the top floor of a private house on Rushton Avenue owned by a schoolteacher named Mrs. Law, a short, gray-haired woman who was as wide as Bubbe. The government required people in the countryside to take in children from London who were being sent to safe areas to escape the bombing. Host families received ten shillings and sixpence a week for an unaccompanied child—about $40 today. Poorer families welcomed the extra income, but after a day spent in a classroom overcrowded with farmers' children and tough little London evacuees, Mrs. Law didn't want to take care of another child from the London slums, and she wouldn't have to if she rented to my mother and me. My mother had secured a clerical position at a tea importing company that had relocated to the countryside. Her salary would more than pay our rent.

We arrived on a Saturday afternoon, carrying our suitcases from the train station to our new home. Mrs. Law showed us around the bleak upstairs flat. The walls were painted pale beige. The living room held an armchair, a small dining table and chairs. A cheap Bakelite radio stood on a tottery side table. We would share a double bed in one of the two bedrooms. The second, tiny bedroom had been turned into a makeshift kitchen with a hotplate, an electric kettle for tea, a small cupboard for storing nonperishables and a big enamel bowl for washing dishes. My mother would have to fill the bowl with water from the bathroom sink. There was no refrigerator or cold storage. Only wealthy people owned refrigerators. Butter, eggs, milk and margarine were stored on top of the cupboard. The temperature rarely went above the low seventies, and if milk went sour we added a little sugar to it and ate it like yogurt. The bathroom held a tub and sink, and the toilet was located in its own small room.

In the living room, an electric fireplace with one glowing bar was the only source of warmth. Its weak heat didn't reach the corners of that room, much less the rest of the apartment. When the weather turned cold, the damp chill seeped into our bones as soon as we moved away from the fireplace. The only way to get really warm in our unheated bedroom was to snuggle into bed with a couple of rubber hot water bottles filled from the teakettle. My mother was always careful to press out the excess air because if you didn't, a bottle might burst in your bed, scalding you badly.

"My nerves are bad," Mrs. Law explained. "I can't tolerate loud noises, so please walk quietly. Always take your shoes off when you come into the house and, if you *must* listen to the wireless, keep the volume down low. I need my rest when I come home."

So my mother and I tiptoed about in our stockinged feet. When Mrs. Law banged a broom handle on the ceiling while we were listening to the crackling radio, we huddled closer with the volume turned down to a whisper. It was hard to hear and I complained bitterly.

"Women in middle age go through something called 'the change,'" my mother explained. "They often have mental problems and become very irritable. That's why she's so disagreeable." When we were in the house, I did my best to keep out of Mrs. Law's way.

On weekends, Mummy and I went for brisk walks to warm ourselves up. But when we came home, my feet were icy, dead-white and numb with cold. I soon developed chilblains on my toes—sore, itchy patches that swelled and festered. My mother smeared them with black, foul-smelling ointment made from fish oil. But it was only the warmth of spring that finally allowed them to heal.

My parents would have preferred to send me to a private school where I would be sheltered from the rough play and coarse manners of farmers' children and working-class evacuees. But there was no private school nearby so I had to attend the state school.

On the first Monday morning after we arrived, my mother and I walked to Godstone Station School, where we met Miss Slatter, the headmistress. There were three classes: Infants (children ages five to seven), Standard One (ages eight to eleven), and Standard Two (twelve to fourteen). I was tested in reading and arithmetic and found to be sadly lacking in the latter. Although I was seven years old, I still didn't know my multiplication tables. Miss Slatter said I should start school the next week, and I was assigned to the lowest class, which happened to be taught by our landlady, Mrs. Law.

Mrs. Law invited me to ride to school with her on my bike, if I had one. I was thrilled, as my parents had given me a two-wheeler for my seventh birthday and Daddy had taught me to ride in our big backyard, holding on to the saddle and running to keep up with me. My father brought the bike down from Croydon on the train that weekend, and on my first day of school I pedaled frantically behind Mrs

Law, following her ample buttocks sagging on either side of her bicycle seat.

As soon as we got to the playground and padlocked our bikes, the bell rang for morning prayers. All state schools were affiliated with the Church of England, and every day began with a religious service. My mother had explained to Miss Slatter that we were Jewish and had asked that I be allowed to stay out of morning prayers. So while the rest of the school prayed and sang hymns, I stood alone outside the assembly room. Daily services consisted of The Lesson—a reading from the New Testament—and hymns in keeping with the season and recent events: "All Things Bright and Beautiful" in the spring; "Eternal Father, Strong to Save" when news from the BBC told us about battles at sea between food convoys and German destroyers; "O Come, O Come, Emmanuel" in the weeks before Christmas; and, of course, carols as Christmas drew near. After prayers, we went to our classrooms. The morning droned on with sing-song repetition of multiplication tables. At Coloma Convent and Miss Cleal's we had recited, "Two twos are four, three twos are six." In Wales they had said, "Two times two is four, three times two is six." Godstone Station School pupils recited their tables like the Welsh. I found the difference in words really confusing and had no idea what they meant, whichever school I attended. No one ever laid out objects to illustrate their meaning. The times tables were just gobbledygook to me. At last, it was reading time. My classmates were struggling to sound out words, but I'd been reading for some time, and I sped through the primers one after another.

When the bell rang for lunchtime recess, we unwrapped our sandwiches, lined up for free milk and ate at our desks. After we finished, we ran out to the playground. Some boys brought marbles out of their pockets and played with them in the dirt. A few boys kicked a soccer ball. Others played conkers, a traditional game played with horse chestnuts.

Horse chestnut trees towered over the edges of fields around the village. In spring they produced upright clusters of pink-and-white flowers that looked like candles. When autumn came, they bore big, nut-like toxic seeds encased in thick green coverings.The boys peeled off the coverings to reveal the shiny horse chestnuts inside, which were ball-shaped and a bit smaller than a ping pong ball. The boys called them conkers.

At recess the boys pulled lengths of string out of their pockets, each one with a nut threaded on it and held in place by a knot at one end of the string. One player let the conker dangle while his opponent swung his conker hard trying to smash the dangler. They continued until one of the conkers broke apart. The winner then tied a knot in his string to mark his victory.

Girls produced jump ropes and skipped to a rhyme that was new to me:

> What ho she jumps.
> She's got the mumps.
> She's got the M. U. M. P. S.

As they shouted out each letter, they turned the rope twice very quickly and jumped high in the air. It looked like fun but my rope was at home.

"Can I play?" I asked.

"Only if you tell us why you don't come to prayers. What are you? Some sort of 'eathen then?"

"No. I'm Jewish and we have different prayers."

"What are they then? Say some."

"*Sh'ma Yisroel, Adonoi eloheynu, Adonoi echod*," I recited, as my mother had taught me.

"Mumbo jumbo, mumbo jumbo," they taunted in a sing-song chorus, pointing fingers. Then they turned their backs and skipped to the other end of the playground and the bell rang for the end of lunch hour.

Back in the classroom, Mrs. Law clapped her hands for silence. "Kneel down everyone. Hands together. Eyes closed."

She stood in front of the class, palms pressed together in front of her enormous bosom. I glanced around at the rest of the children. They all knelt next to their desks, so I did the same. Perhaps this was going to be a physical education lesson, I thought.

"Our Father," Mrs. Law began, "which art in heaven…."

I scrambled to my feet and back into my seat as if the floor were red hot and my knees had been burned.

Mrs. Law, hearing my chair scrape, opened her eyes, scarily enlarged behind thick glasses. She clapped her hands again.

"One minute, everyone."

The voices trailed off in mid-sentence.

"Cynthia Shelower. What *do* you think you're doing? Get back down on your knees. This minute!"

"I can't." I murmured.

"What did you say? Speak up, child."

"I can't," I said a bit louder.

"And why not, pray tell?"

"I'm Jewish and we don't kneel to pray. And that's not our prayer. My mummy says I'm not allowed to pray Christian prayers."

Heads twisted in my direction, as 36 pairs of eyes turned toward me.

"I never heard of such a thing. You'd better sit in your chair and be quiet then," Mrs. Law said, wagging her head from side to side. "Now class, settle down. Hands together. Eyes closed."

I felt fire in my cheeks as I sat conspicuously high above the rest of the kneeling pupils. The recitation seemed endless but at last they reached, "For thine is the kingdom, the power and the glory, for ever and ever. Amen."

In the afternoon, Mrs. Law read us a chapter of *Peter Pan*. Then monitors handed out crayons and colored construction paper and we made drawings as best we could. The five-year-olds scribbled designs. I drew a house with trees on either side of it. I longed to go home to Croydon.

Finally, the bell rang and we grabbed our coats off hooks at the back of the room. I undid the padlock on my bike and started to pedal back to our flat as fast as I could. I knew the way: a straight path bordered by beds of stinging nettles—a bushy green plant with barbed leaves that sting the skin and raise a painful rash. As I rode, I heard voices and glanced over my shoulder. Three boys from the oldest class were behind me. I hoped there was enough room for them to pass without my having to steer into the nettles.

Suddenly, a boy rode his bicycle across the path in front of me, blocking my way. The other two pushed me off my bike, and one grabbed hold of my arm.

"I've got 'er. 'Old 'er 'ands be'oind 'er."

The biggest boy twisted my arm up behind my back. I could smell the ripeness of him: unwashed clothes and body and a whiff of manure from the hobnailed soles of his boots. A blond boy took out his jacknife, opened it and pressed the point against the front of my coat.

"Let's feel then," he said. "I know Jews 'ave 'orns." He rubbed his hand roughly over the top of my head. "Nah," he sneered. "'Ers 'aven't grown in yet."

They pushed me against the hedge and the nettles stung my bare legs like a swarm of wasps. I tried to scream but no sound came out, just a rasping breath. The blond boy pushed his knife further into the front of my coat and slashed through the two top buttonholes. Then they jumped onto their bikes and rode away.

I pulled my bike out of the nettles, stinging my hands in the process, and rode to Rushton Avenue, my coat flapping open, crying all the way.

Chapter 13
Misfits

The next day, my mother walked with me to school to see Miss Slatter. She held up my slashed coat and described my tearful homecoming.

Miss Slatter listened, nodding. "Well, you'll have to expect a bit of reaction from the farm children," she said. "They've never met a Jew before and Cynthia does put on airs."

"Put on airs?" my mother said, shocked. "What do you mean?"

"Isn't that the school uniform from her old school?" Miss Slatter said, pointing to my navy blue coat with a badge on the pocket. "We don't wear uniforms. This is a council school. People don't parade their finery here."

"But this is the only coat she has," my mother protested. "I can't afford to buy Cynthia new school outfits."

Miss Slatter shrugged. "Boys will be boys, you know. If Cynthia can tell me which children were involved, I'll have a word with them."

"Do you know their names?" my mother asked.

"No Mummy. I don't know anyone's name yet." I was about to say I knew their faces, but Miss Slatter cut me off.

"That's too bad," she said. "Let's just try to put this behind us, then, Mrs. Shelower, shall we?"

"That was a complete waste of time," Mummy muttered as we left.

"Should I tell Mrs. Law?" I asked.

"No, Cynthia, I don't think that would be helpful. You'd better just try to keep out of their way."

My mother's job at the tea importers was about three miles from our house. She bought herself a second-hand bicycle and rode it to work, where she was able to get a hot lunch in the office canteen. This mattered enormously because we didn't have a proper kitchen in our upstairs flat. To make sure I also had at least one nourishing meal a day, she arranged for me to eat lunch at The Railway Hotel opposite school.

"But the food's not kosher there," I said. "Should I ask for vegetarian?"

"No, dear," my mother replied. "Just eat what they serve you. Don't worry about eating kosher. The Chief Rabbi has told us that because of the war, we can eat nonkosher meals if we have to. We just have to avoid eating pork and shellfish and I've asked the people at the hotel not to serve them to you. It's more important to keep healthy than to keep kosher during wartime."

The other children brought sandwiches to school that they ate in our classroom, so when I ate lunch at the hotel, I was, again, singled out as different.

After two weeks in the Infants' class, I was moved up to the next level. Our teacher was Miss Britton, a tall, pale-faced young woman with brown hair cut in the currently popular shingle style, almost as short as a boy's. There were 45 of us in this class: children of farmers and laborers together with London evacuees.

Several children from poor local families came to school surrounded by a foul aroma almost thick enough to touch: a combination of dirty clothes, unwashed bodies and hair, dried urine and the barnyard. Two of them, Nancy Williams and Ernie Brown, were particularly aromatic, their hands and legs grimy and streaked with dirt. Nancy had matted blond hair and protruding teeth with a greenish tinge, and Ernie's head was cropped close, probably in an attempt to repel lice and ringworm. Miss Britton tried to be extra kind to Ernie and Nancy, which only increased the other children's dislike for them.

They became the objects of a cruel game. If a classmate accidentally touched Nancy or Ernie, they would go up and touch the nearest person and whisper, "Brown Touch" or "Williams Touch." That person, in turn, would find someone to pass the touch along to, each child shuddering with mock horror at having had even pass-along contact with one of the pariahs.

I felt sorry for Nancy and Ernie, but I wanted so much to be accepted and make friends that I joined in the game. But just as Ernie and Nancy were singled out for being poor, dirty and smelly, I also continued to be singled out for being different and "putting on airs." I still wore the coat from my old school uniform, I spoke more refined English than the other children did and I loved to perform. At Christmas, when the school held a talent show, I stood on a chair, sang and did impersonations of people on radio comedy shows. I was delighted with the applause, and when my classmates asked me to do impersonations on the playground afterwards, I was quick to comply. But when I finished performing, the other children turned their backs on me, calling me a show-off. They still refused to include me in their games. And, of course, I still didn't attend morning prayers. My mother complained again to Miss Slatter about the way I was being treated but she was not sympathetic.

Godstone Station School was very different from Coloma Convent. Our classroom was heated by a pot-bellied stove, and a wheezing harmonium—a small reed organ— stood in one corner. We sat at old desks, ink-blotched and gouged with initials. At first we wrote in pencil on both sides of speckly recycled paper. When we learned to write cursive, we dipped our scratchy pen nibs into white china inkwells lined with a thin crust of ancient dried ink and nested into hollows at the top of our desks. The paper was so thin and absorbent, the ink bled through to the other side. We were told not to stay within margins on the page but to fill the paper up as much as we could. Britain had virtually no forests to supply the raw material for paper. Before the war, wood pulp had been imported from Norway. Now there was a severe shortage and paper was being rationed and recycled. Newspapers had to reduce the number of pages they printed. Being frugal with writing paper was part of our contribution to the war effort.

Miss Britton was also hard pressed to find enough reading material for everyone because the school was hosting so many evacuees. She managed to find paper-bound copies of an abridged version of *Lorna Doone*. Many of the children in my class were just beginning to read and they struggled to sound out the words. I was intrigued by the dark romance and followed the tale of Lorna Doone and John Ridd's clandestine love affair with great interest. When I read how the villain, Carver Doone, was sucked into quicksand, his horrible death haunted my dreams. On rainy days, the fields near our house turned muddy and I was terrified of being sucked below.

A couple of months after I moved up to the next level in school, Miss Britton quit teaching to join the WAAFs—the Women's Auxiliary Air Force. Our next teacher was Mrs. Jacobs, a middle-aged retired opera singer who believed in teaching what she knew best. She skimmed over our reading, writing and arithmetic lessons and taught us how to sing. My favorite part of the day came when she sat down at the creaky harmonium. We breathed from our diaphragms, practiced scales and arpeggios and sang "Cherry Ripe," "When April Sings" and "The Lass of Richmond Hill," trying to sound like Deanna Durbin, the miraculous young soprano movie star.

Mrs. Jacobs also taught us how to knit. The boys were clumsy with their needles and protested that knitting was for girls, but Mrs. Jacobs insisted they were making a meaningful contribution to the war effort. So, with much grumbling, they joined us in making scarves, balaclavas and gloves for soldiers, sailors and airmen. Some of the gloves were made without fingers so the wearers would be able to handle guns with dexterity. The balaclavas enveloped the whole head and neck, leaving an opening for the face. Some khaki and navy blue yarn was handed out in school but many of us brought yarn from home, where we unraveled old hand-knitted sweaters and washed the wool so it was good as new.

Chapter 14
Country Life

A s Spring 1941 approached, we spent time each day on the playground preparing for the school's May Day celebrations, learning traditional Morris dances and dancing around a maypole while a wind-up phonograph played scratchy folk tunes at full volume. Every student held a colored ribbon attached at the opposite end to the top of the pole, and as we twirled and skipped around one another the ribbons braided and unbraided. During the final dance, called "The Spider's Web," the ribbons wove an openwork colored net above our heads. The boys entered into this activity under duress. Dancing was for sissies, they said.

Coloma Convent and Miss Cleal's had been all-girls schools, and before I went to Godstone Station School I'd met very few boys. I found their behavior strange and a little scary. They didn't hold proper conversations like the girls, and seemed to use very few real words; instead, they made lots of noises imitating airplanes, guns or bomb explosions, interspersed with farting sounds bubbling from their lips. The boys were rough and hit each other a lot. They wore shabby-looking V-necked sweaters and short pants, and their hobnailed boots struck sparks when they ran. I tried to stay out of their way.

My mother hated living in the country. She complained that there was nothing to do in South Godstone—no shops, cinemas or theaters. She especially missed theater. She still loved it and had attended as often as possible before the war. The village gossip and lack of privacy aggravated her, too. When we took the train to Redhill, the nearest major town, for a day of shopping and a movie, people in the village would ask how we had enjoyed our trip and she felt this was an invasion of privacy, not a friendly question. She was sure the nosy postmistress steamed our letters open. With only one general store in the village, she struggled to get food on the table – especially on weekends, when we weren't able to eat a hot lunch. Also, we had no chickens so we were back to two eggs per person per week. She tried valiantly to come up with concoctions she could prepare on the hotplate and found a recipe in a government pamphlet for an uncooked chocolate cake that became our regular weekend dessert.

Our escape from the Blitz was by no means total. Godstone and South Godstone were in the general flight path from Germany to Croydon and other RAF airfields. German bomber pilots sometimes missed their targets or were fought off by anti-aircraft fire and dropped their incendiary bombs and high explosives in the fields around us before returning to base. Thankfully, they usually avoided or missed the houses, but many nights we were awakened by air-raid sirens and loud explosions. My mother and I clung together when this happened. "They're bombing the cows," she'd say, trying to sound lighthearted as the house shook and trembled around us. We learned to avoid the bomb craters in the fields and were warned regularly in school not to go near unexploded bombs or pick up shells or other metal objects which often lay hidden by waving wheat or tall grasses. Newspapers often printed stories about children who had discovered and played with these devices and been badly maimed or killed. In spite of these warnings, most boys collected pieces of shrapnel that they showed proudly to one another at recess.

There were no community shelters in South Godstone but we did have a concrete building on the playground at school. On the rare occasions when there were daytime raids we moved into this shelter, where Mrs. Jacobs tried to keep our spirits up by teaching us songs. These included a version of "Baa Baa Blacksheep" in French.

Baa baa mouton noir
Avez-vous de laine?
Oui monsieur, oui monsieur,
Trois sacs pleins.

I was puzzled by her choice of a French song since none of us was ever going to learn French at Godstone Station School.

While my mother complained about living in South Godstone, I found some things to enjoy in the country. I kept my opinions to myself. Letting her know there were things I loved about the countryside would have seemed like a betrayal.

Twice a week, I walked half a mile to Scott's Farm carrying a miniature milk churn. I gave sixpence to Mrs. Scott—about $2.00 today—and she filled the churn with milk, still warm from the cow. Classmates told me the names of wildflowers growing in the hedgerows: magenta ragged-robin, purple vetch, scarlet pimpernel, electric-blue speedwell and one we called bacon and eggs because of its stripey yellow and vermillion flowers. I would pick bunches to decorate our table.

My mother had no love for gardening and neither did Mrs. Law, so our front yard was woefully neglected, filled with wild orange wallflowers and rambling pink-flowered bindweed vines climbing all over the wall. Our neighbors, however, took meticulous care of their flower beds. In their gardens, lavender grew in huge bushes, purple aubrieta and blue lobelia cascaded over banks, and miniature columbines poked delicately through cracks in rocks.

In the spring, my mother and I walked in the woods near our house. Carpets of bluebells interspersed with yellow primroses and violets filled the air with sweet scents. Even in her misery, my mother grudgingly admired the beauty that surrounded us.

As spring edged toward summer, my mother heard nightingales singing outside our window in the evening. She was entranced and let me stay up late on weekends to listen. Unlike other birds, the nightingale didn't repeat any musical phrase. He was like a joyful opera singer performing his entire repertoire. I reread Hans Christian Andersen's story "The Nightingale" and shared the author's dislike of the king who preferred a mechanical bird in a cage to the real one singing outside his window. My mother was so intrigued by the nightingale's serenade, she wrote to her sister Fan, a true lover of beauty, inviting her for the weekend so she could hear it. Fan seemed to enjoy her visit, but Mum was disappointed when she nodded off to sleep before the nightingale began to sing, missing the whole concert.

At the end of my first school year in South Godstone, Mrs. Law retired from teaching and moved away, and we took over her downstairs flat. We still only had one bedroom, so my mother and I continued sharing the bed. I was moved to the sofa when my father came down on leave. Living downstairs gave us direct access to the big backyard, where I was able to start my own garden plot. I planted lettuce, radishes and rutabagas, which we called swedes. Before the war, swedes had been cattle food, but now everyone ate them. When they were mashed with a little margarine and grated nutmeg, they became one of my favorite vegetables. My father planted tomatoes when he came for the weekend, and while only a few of them ripened in the rainy English summer, the rest weren't wasted because my mother made delicious green tomato chutney and we often ate cheese and chutney sandwiches for our tea.

Now that we had a big backyard, my parents decided to raise hens just like they had in Croydon. When my mother and I moved to South Godstone, my father sold our Croydon hens to the kosher butcher. Now, in South Godstone, he built a new chicken house and brought in a set of young pullets: Rhode Island Reds and White Wyandottes. Once again, eggs became a staple part of our diet.

When the wheat at the end of our road was ready for harvest, the farmer brought in a combine harvester that gathered, threshed and winnowed, separating wheat from chaff. After the harvest was done and wheat was stacked in huge sheaves in the field, he gave us rides on the hay cart. One day, my mother said, "Come on, Cynthia. Let's go gleaning." I smiled. Just like Ruth in the Bible, I thought.

For my eighth birthday, my parents had given me a copy of the King James Bible illustrated with reproductions of famous paintings, including Rembrandt's portrait of Ruth. I had read her story over and over and remembered that she had gone to "glean and gather among the sheaves behind the reapers."

My mother took the big enamel basin we used for washing dishes and we walked through the field picking up wheat stalks the combine harvester had left behind—an extra treat for the chickens in our backyard. It was a beautiful day, and as much as my mother insisted she hated living in the country, she looked happy walking through the field. I wanted the day to last forever.

Once again, my father's order for female chicks had included a Rhode Island Red cockerel by mistake. He grew into a handsome fellow with an upright, bright red cockscomb on top of his head and generous wattles waggling under his chin. One day, he started attacking a hen, kicking her with his strong, spurred feet and pecking at her eyes. He was soon joined by the rest of the flock, which chased the hen all over the run, pecking and trapping her in a corner. My mother and I tried shouting and banging saucepan lids together like cymbals to scare them off but nothing would dissuade them and we stood by, helpless, watching the flock attack the poor hen. When my father came on leave the next day, he removed the injured chicken from the henhouse, but she was almost dead by the time she was rescued. We brought her inside, put her in a cardboard box with a hot water bottle and tried to feed her with a medicine dropper. Daddy dabbed at her bloody wounds with cotton balls dipped in disinfectant while I stroked her feathers; but she was past help. I was inconsolable when my father took her into the backyard and wrung her neck.

Seeing how distraught I was, Daddy patted his knee. "Come and sit here," he said. I settled on his lap and lay my head on his chest. "I know it's sad and it seems cruel, but chickens don't know any other way to behave."

"It's awful," I said. "They're so mean to one another."

"Yes. It is mean," he agreed. "But chickens have something called the pecking order. The cockerel decides who is the weakest hen in the flock and he starts to torment her. He's the leader and all the other hens follow him. See how tiny their heads are? They have very small brains so they can't think for themselves."

"But it's not right. It's as if they're killing members of their own family."

"It does seem wrong. But that's the way chickens are made. People sometimes behave that way, too. Just think about Hitler. He has persuaded the Germans to follow him and carry out cruel policies persecuting people. But here in England we think for ourselves. That's why there's a war on."

I shifted uncomfortably on his lap. I couldn't help thinking about Nancy Williams and Ernie Brown and the Touch game.

My parents decided to put the poor hen out of her misery. They also decided we should eat her, even though she wouldn't be kosher: not only would she not be killed in the ritual manner but her body was also not healthy and whole as required. Mummy explained that it was wartime, food was scarce, and the Chief Rabbi had said it was OK to bend the rules. The hen was food, kosher or not. From my parents' point of view, it would have been unthinkable just to discard her.

My mother was accustomed to buying chickens from the kosher butcher and bringing them home almost ready to cook. This time my parents had to do everything themselves. Daddy took the hen outside to wring her neck and pluck her, and Mummy spent over an hour cleaning her and removing the last few feathers with tweezers. But my mother had no experience drawing chickens— pulling out their innards. Chickens from the butcher came cleaned inside and out. Tentatively, she slit the hen between its legs, poked two dainty fingers into the cavity and started to pull. When a single bloody entrail wiggled out, she recoiled with a little scream. She washed her hands and rubbed lotion on them. Then she put on a pair of rubber gloves, laid the chicken on a plate and put the plate on top of an upside-down saucepan with a bowl next to it. Gingerly, tears pouring down her face,

Mum pulled the intestines, hand over hand, into the bowl using a finger and thumb. I watched from a slight distance, fascinated by the never-ending string of bloody entrails.

Suddenly, she turned on me with uncharacteristic fury and screamed, "Get out of the kitchen! Get out!"

I retreated to the doorway but continued watching, mesmerized, until ten feet or so of slimy intestines were piled in the bowl. My mother buried her head in her arms and sobbed. Years later, I learned that a ritual slaughterer would have slit the bird, stuck his hand inside the body, grasped the innards and pulled them all out together in one deft movement.

We continued to keep chickens for their eggs, but my mother avoided cooking or eating chicken after that.

Tilly's Green Tomato Chutney *(Makes about 8 pints)*
- 1 quart cider or malt vinegar
- 1 pound brown sugar
- ½ teaspoon cayenne pepper
- 4 pounds green tomatoes, chopped
- ¾ pound onions, peeled and diced
- 1 medium-sized head garlic, all cloves peeled and sliced thin
- 2 pounds apples (Granny Smith or Rhode Island Greening), peeled, cored and chopped
- 1 pound raisins
- 10 dry chili peppers tied in a cheesecloth
- 2 tablespoons salt

1. Add all ingredients to an 8-quart stockpot. Stir to combine. Bring to a boil.
2. Lower heat and simmer, stirring occasionally, until mixture has reduced and thickened to the consistency of jam – at least one hour.
3. Discard the bag of chilli peppers and allow the mixture to cool.
4. Ladle thickened mixture into sterilized jars. Place waxpaper over top of jar before tightening lid to enhance seal and prevent corrosion (optional).
5. Store in a cool, dry place. Refrigerate after opening.
This chutney can be enjoyed immediately but improves with age and is best after 3 months. It makes a good hostess gift and can be stored for about two years.

Uncooked Chocolate Cake
- 2 ounces margarine
- 2 ounces sugar
- 2 tablespoons golden syrup (a British staple)
- 2 ounces cocoa powder
- 1 teaspoon vanilla extract
- 6 ounces crisp breadcrumbs

1. To make the breadcrumbs, let bread get very stale and grate on a grater.
2. Put margarine, sugar and syrup into a saucepan and heat gently until the margarine has melted.
3. Remove from heat and stir in the cocoa powder, vanilla and breadcrumbs. Mix well.
4. Grease a 7" x 7" square cake tin with margarine. Pour and press the mixture into the pan.
5. Let stand for 4 to 5 hours until firm, then turn out carefully.

Icing
- 2 teaspoons melted margarine
- 1 tablespoon cocoa powder
- I tablespoon golden syrup
- ½ teaspoon vanilla extract

1. Mix together melted margarine, cocoa powder, syrup and vanilla.
2. Spread on cake.

Chapter 15
Playmates

We rolled around in the white fluffy seeds of Old Man's Beard trees, piled like feathers on the ground. Angela and I were playing mothers and fathers. We were both eight years old, but she was a couple of months older, so she was the mother and I was the baby. She sprinkled me with the downy fluff as she put me to bed in a small hollow next to the ditch and fed me pretend sips of warm milk, a delicious nightcap before I lay down to sleep. Leafy branches met overhead and made our secret place feel just like a real house. We had gathered acorns, separating them into wrinkled cups and shiny nuts, and collected small stones to build a fireplace, where Angela busied herself cooking tomorrow's soup: acorns and fallen leaves thrown into her school satchel and stirred with a stick. While the phantom soup simmered, she plopped down on the ground and pretended to write a letter to her husband, my daddy, in the army somewhere in Europe.

Angela was an evacuee like me. Her actual dad was in the army, and her mother was working in a munitions factory back in London. I was lucky because my mother and I lived in the village together, and my father came to visit whenever he had three days' leave. Even though Angela had a cockney accent, she was the closest match I could find to my friends from home. The other girls jumped rope or played ball games during recess. Angela was the only one who liked to play pretend games like I did. She wasn't rough like the other London children or farmers' kids who constantly picked fights on the playground and pushed when we stood in line.

The evacuees were mostly tough kids from London's poor East End who had been sent away from their families and didn't know when they'd see their parents again. Some were billeted with villagers, some with local farming families, and others with landed gentry who'd opened their homes to the children as part of "doing their bit" for the war effort. Angela and her four-year-old sister, Mary, lived with Mr. and Mrs. Anderson and their live-in maid, Gladys, in an imposing house on the outskirts of the village. The Andersons had no children of their own and had welcomed the siblings warmly.

We felt a few drops of rain, gathered up our belongings and ran home. I walked through the front door and slipped off my shoes. My mother took one look at my coat, covered in fluffy seeds, and exploded.

"Don't you know that clothes are rationed? How can I get your coat cleaned? There are no dry cleaners here. There's only one lousy shop in this godforsaken place. Find the clothes brush. How am I ever going to get this stuff off?"

I hung my head and started looking for the brush in the tall chest of drawers in the bedroom we shared.

"I'm sorry, Mummy." I said. "We were playing and I forgot to take it off."

When the wheat ripened and rippled in the breeze in the fields at the end of our road, Angela and I would play a kind of hide-and-seek. Lying flat on our stomachs, we'd wriggle along the ground, flattening the wheat stalks. Sometimes our paths crossed and we found each other. If we didn't, we would call out and stand up, often surprised to find that we were so close.

One day, Angela invited me to the Andersons' house to play. My mother told me to mind my manners. I was to say "please" and "thank you" and refuse second helpings of cake even if they were pressed upon me. Most important, when leaving, I was to remember to say, "Thank you for having me."

I walked up the path leading to the Andersons' front door through a beautiful garden where a small pond was surrounded by yellow irises. Mrs. Anderson welcomed me warmly before Angela and I went upstairs together to the pretty bedroom she shared with her sister. We sat down on her bed. "Wait 'ere," she said and ran out of the room. She came back carrying a huge book called *Lives of the Saints*, illustrated with reproductions of famous paintings. Angela giggled behind her hand. "Look at this one," she said. A cherubic baby Jesus sat on his mother's lap, naked. Angela showed me how if we looked closely, we could get a glimpse of his tiny penis. We laughed at it together. Just then, we heard Mrs. Anderson's footsteps on the stairs and Angela snapped the book shut.

"You have a lovely surprise downstairs, Angela," Mrs. Anderson said. "You'll never guess who's come to see you."

The living room was furnished with chintz-covered sofas and overstuffed armchairs. Vases filled with sweet-smelling roses were on the coffee table and grand piano and sun streamed in through the French doors. Sitting on the edge of a chair with her hands clasped together was a woman dressed in a worn brown skirt and a creased, cream-colored blouse. A flattened beret was perched on one side of her head, and a lumpy handbag and zippered carryall sat on the floor beside her.

"Mum!" Angela cried. Her mother stood and Angela ran up to her and clasped her around the waist. "Ooh Mum. 'Ave you come to tyke us 'ome?"

"Nah, lovey," the woman answered. "I was able to get a lift on the back of a lorry, so I just come down for the day. Where's our Mary?"

Mrs. Anderson entered through the French doors. "Here's Mary," she said. Mary, skinny with wispy blond hair and huge green eyes, had a thumb stuck firmly in her mouth. She clung to Mrs. Anderson's hand and hid behind her skirt. Then she took her thumb out of her mouth. "Are you the nice lady who's come down from London to see me?" Mary asked.

Suddenly, Angela's mother let out a wail. "She don't know me no more," she sobbed. "She don't know me no more."

Mrs. Anderson turned to me, a worried look on her face. "It's time for you to go home now, dear," she said. "Your Mummy will be expecting you."

I remembered to say, "Thank you for having me," and ran all the way home.

Cynthia Ehrenkrantz

Chapter 16
Austerity

I rang the bell of another grand-looking house not far from the center of South Godstone village. It was opened by a woman wearing a tweed skirt, a navy blue twinset, a string of pearls and matching earrings. "Please, Miss, do you have any silver paper?" I asked.

The school had asked us to take part in a salvage drive, and I was grasping a small ball of aluminum foil, saved from candy and food wrappers.

"Let me see what I can find," the woman said.

I waited in the hallway where a bowl of multicolored flowers sat on a long table, filling the air with heavy perfume. A few minutes later, she came back and gave me a paper bag filled with scraps of thin silver foil. My house-to-house solicitations would add several layers to the shiny little ball I would bring into school on Monday—my personal, proud contribution to the war effort.

Everyone in South Godstone was doing their bit. We saved aluminum foil to be sent to munitions factories. We wrote on both sides of speckly, spongy paper even though ink bled through and made our writing hard to read. My mother greased pie pans with the dabs of butter and margarine that clung to wrappers she kept in an old cookie tin to use up every scrap of our food rations. We saved soap slivers in a glass jar, shook them up with warm water and used the liquid for laundry. When a jar of jam was finished, Mum filled it with water, shook it, and I drank it as if it were a fruit-flavored beverage.

Clothes rationing had begun in June 1941. By this point in the war, one fourth of the population was wearing some kind of uniform so facilities for making civilian clothes were very limited. Clothes were designed according to strict guidelines and called Utility Clothing. To conserve fabric, men's trousers had no cuffs, women's skirts were shortened, and all garments had fewer pockets and buttons. My mother let down sleeves and hems so I could wear my clothes longer, even though I was growing fast, and they were tight across the shoulders and chest. If there wasn't enough material to lengthen a dress, she added scraps in a contrasting color to make a false hem. I felt no embarrassment wearing such dowdy clothes; all the girls at school were dressed like me.

Our pencils had no erasers on the ends and were made of plain wood, not painted on the outside. In school, we used wax crayons that felt rough on the paper. You couldn't draw fine lines with them, and the color came off on your hand.

I loved coloring and drawing. For my eighth birthday, along with the Bible, Mum had decided to buy me a whole new set of colored pencils and walked into the village store to purchase them.

"Sorry, ma'am," the shopkeeper said. "They only sent us yellow. We didn't get any other colors."

The following Saturday, she took the train to Redhill and spent the afternoon trekking from shop to shop, buying a red pencil at one store, a blue one at another, until finally she gathered a whole set: red, blue, yellow, black, green, brown and orange. I was thrilled to get them and spent many hours on the sheepskin rug in front of the fire, drawing pictures. I was an untidy child who never put my toys away and left everything scattered on the rug after each coloring session.

"Cynthia," my mother said as she gathered up drawings and pencils for the umpteenth time. "If you leave these out again, I'm going to throw them on the fire. You *must* learn to put your toys away." She laid the pencils neatly in a square tin with a picture of Princesses Elizabeth and Margaret on the lid and snapped it shut.

I pouted and sighed. There were so many things to do that were much more interesting than putting away toys.

A few days later, I left the pencils and artwork on the rug as usual.

"What did I say I was going to do with those things if you left them out again?" my mother asked.

I burst into tears, gathered up my beloved pencils and threw them into the fire. My mother gasped and almost screamed. She told me later she'd worn out too much shoe leather collecting the pencils to even consider destroying them—and that I was a most obedient child who took care of my punishment before she could. She also admitted I'd taught her an important lesson: never make empty threats. For myself, I was just tired of her badgering and it was my way of ending her nagging.

The most noticeable shortages became apparent in the way we ate. The only unrationed foods were bread, fish, potatoes, coffee, fruits and vegetables, and these were in limited supply. Everyone who had the tiniest patch of garden tried growing their own vegetables.

People were nostalgic about foods that were no longer obtainable. My mother described asparagus to me, telling me it wasn't like any other vegetable. It was cooked standing up in the pot so the tips didn't get overdone. And it was the only vegetable well-bred people were allowed to eat with their fingers, picking up the spears by the stem and dipping them in melted butter. Hearing about it was like listening to a fairytale.

We had no bananas. My mother described them and showed me pictures in books. "Such a delicious fruit," she said. "And so convenient too. When you peeled one, the skin made a perfect holder. Your hands didn't get sticky like they do when you eat an apple or a pear." She sighed. "I used to love cantaloupe, too," she continued. "Most people threw the seeds away but I loved nibbling on them. They were like little tiny nuts."

Onions were still in short supply. British farmers had begun growing onions but they were a much-prized vegetable. Some were raffled at church bazaars or brought to friends' houses as hostess gifts.

People didn't complain much about rationing, though, because it seemed a fair way to distribute food and make sure everyone had enough at a time when supplies were scarce. Two ounces of tea per person per week was a true hardship, and housewives tore open their tea packets to extract the last tiny leaves hiding in the creases. But even the landed gentry weren't entitled to any more rations than we were, and we took comfort in believing news reports that the Royal Family had to make do with food shortages just like us. Bread and milk were considered essential foods and were subsidized by the government to keep prices down. Children from poor families actually ate better under rationing than they had before.

Standing in long lines for food became the standard method of shopping. We called it "queueing up," an expression that became popular during the war. Before that, we never used it to mean "standing in line." A queue was the name for a Chinese man's pigtail. I once heard a friend of my mother's who was hard of hearing pronounce it *kweewee*, as she'd never heard the word spoken while she could still hear.

Sometimes an imported fruit would become available and signs would appear in the window of the greengrocers:

Oranges—One to a Customer. My mother would join the queue and, when she'd received her quota, take off her hat and get in line again. If it wasn't raining, she would hand me her coat and queue up a third time. Once the greengrocer looked her in the eye and said, "'Aven't you been 'ere already, Mum?"

"Cawse not," she replied in a phony cockney accent, pretending to be very offended.

Many of our evening meals came from tins: Heinz baked beans or canned spaghetti on toast were often served for supper. Sometimes my mother would make a salad with sliced cabbage, grated turnips and carrots. And then there were pilchards—fish canned in tomato sauce. Larger than sardines and smaller than herrings, they had mushy bones and a gritty texture. And that sauce! Yuck! Its metallic taste stayed with me for several hours. Pilchards were supposed to be another name for sardines. But these grayish-beige creatures in curdled-looking sauce dotted with oily globules bore no resemblance to the silky little fish nestled in olive oil that I loved.

I looked forward to my father's visits because my mother would make special vegetarian dishes he and I both loved. Her macaroni and cheese was enhanced by the addition of a little dry mustard, and she sometimes made her mother's potato soup.

The government constantly warned people not to waste food. My mother never even threw away the water in which she'd boiled vegetables. She saved it to use as vegetable stock for soup.

A short daily radio program called *The Kitchen Front* came on six mornings a week right after the eight o'clock news and featured people talking about food, providing recipes and kitchen hints.

Cartoon characters named Potato Pete and Doctor Carrot appeared in leaflets, posters and advertisements encouraging people to consume more of these two vegetables, which were plentiful. We were urged to eat at least one potato a day and assured that eating carrots would improve our eyesight. We were told the reason RAF pilots did so well at spotting and bringing down enemy bombers at night was because they ate lots of carrots. The real reason was a new secret technology called radar that we didn't learn about until later.

The Food Ministry published pamphlets filled with recipes that relied on vegetables rather than meat or fish. Lord Woolton was the Minister of Food and was warmly regarded as people believed his rationing program was fair. But a vegetable-based pot-pie-like concoction called Lord Woolton Pie, developed by the chef of the Savoy Hotel, was not popular. Woolton Pie was made with cooked cauliflower, carrots, rutabagas and potatoes, thickened with oatmeal and flavored with vegetable extract. The pastry was made with whole wheat flour, margarine and mashed potatoes. Newspapers published the recipe widely and people made and ate it because it was nutritious and used vegetables that were easy to obtain, but most people found it tasteless and bland, even by British standards. Many said it tasted like cardboard.

One day, my mother came across a recipe for a mock banana sandwich spread made with parnsips, banana extract and sugar. I tried it but didn't like it one bit. If this was what bananas tasted like, I wondered what all the fuss was about.

No one had any money to spare. It didn't matter much because there was virtually nothing to spend it on. My father's weekly wage as a fireman covered the bulk of our regular expenses but left nothing over to save for a rainy day. Before the war, my parents' business had often struggled and they had disagreed about how it should be run. My mother was frugal, cautious and penny-pinching; my father was a risk taker, extravagant and bad at handling cash flow. They had argued a lot. When my father closed the business and joined the Fire Service, the quarrels stopped. Ironically, their marriage seemed to thrive in wartime. Living in South Godstone, I could sense my mother's excitement when Daddy was coming for a three-day leave. When he was with us, the house was often filled with laughter.

One weekend evening after I had gone to bed, I was surprised to hear them quarrelling downstairs. Their loud voices triggered dim, unpleasant memories of arguments before the war and my stomach started turning. I bit my lip and screwed my eyes tight shut, trying to hold back tears.

They were arguing because my father had gone to an auction and bought a job-lot of antique china and a John Broadwood Concert Grand Piano for four pounds, about $280.00 today. "Such a good deal," I could hear him say. "When you come back to Croydon, I'll play for you and Cynthia will be able to have piano lessons. It was a steal."

"A steal?" Mum screeched. "What kind of a steal is that? A bomb could drop on the house and everything you bought could be destroyed in an instant. How am I supposed to buy groceries if you've spent all your pay?" Her voice was shrill and teary. The next morning they sat silently at the breakfast table. When my father left for the railroad station there were no hugs, kisses or fond good-byes.

For the next couple of weeks, we ate lots of pilchards and baked beans on toast for supper.

Lord Woolton Pie —The Official Recipe (as published in
The Times, April 26, 1941)
Take 1 lb. each diced of potatoes, cauliflower, swedes,
and carrots, three or four spring onions—if possible, one
teaspoonful of vegetable extract, and one tablespoonful
of oatmeal. Cook all together for 10 minutes with just
enough water to cover. Stir occasionally to prevent the
mixture from sticking. Allow to cool; put into a pie dish,
sprinkle with chopped parsley, and cover with a crust of
potato or wheatmeal pastry. Bake in a moderate oven
until the pastry is nicely browned and serve hot with a
brown gravy.

Mock Banana Sandwich Spread
• 3 large parsnips, peeled and chopped
• 1-2 tablespoons or more superfine sugar
• ½ teaspoon or more banana extract

1. Boil parsnips 5-10 minutes until soft.
2. Drain and mash.
3. Add sugar and banana extract and mix.
4. Continue mashing and adjusting flavor to desired
consistency and taste.

Chapter 17
Pets

"Do you know how Judy is doing at Mrs. Chapman's?" I asked my mother.

We were in our kitchen in South Godstone. My mother had snapped open her powder compact and was putting on lipstick, getting ready to leave for work.

"I'm sure she's just fine, dear. Hurry up and eat your egg or you'll be late for school."

I sliced the top off my soft-boiled egg, dipped the spoon in and licked yolk off the tip.

Mrs. Chapman had been our cleaning lady in Croydon. Before we moved to South Godstone, Mrs. Law had said, "No dogs allowed." Daddy was too busy at the fire station to take care of Judy so my mother said she would take her to stay with Mrs. Chapman. Judy was a year older than I, and she'd been my playmate for as long as I could remember. A spaniel-mutt, she was affectionate and intelligent. When I complained to Judy about perceived injustices or a mean teacher, she cocked her head to one side and gazed at me with limpid brown eyes. She seemed to understand everything. I'd been sad when Mummy walked out the door with her and came back alone but she assured me that it would only be for a little while. "Until things calm down and we can move back."

I missed having a pet. Mrs. Law had a green parakeet who could actually talk. Sometimes when I got home from school before my mother arrived from work, Mrs. Law would let me sit in her living room to watch him hopping about in his cage. She took her bird with her when she moved away, and I was delighted when my mother presented me with a blue parakeet a few months later. I named him Joey and taught him to say his name and "Pretty Bird." He greeted us every day when we came home from work or school by fluttering off his perch, grasping the bars of his cage with tiny toes and chirping at us. We let him out in the evenings and he sat on my shoulder, pecking ever so gently at birdseed I'd put there for him.

One evening, while my mother washed dishes in the kitchen, Joey landed on the living room mantel next to a small pitcher filled with wild flowers. I put out my hand for him to hop onto and accidentally knocked the pitcher over. It fell onto the hearth, breaking into three pieces. I crept into the bathroom, grabbed a towel to mop up the mess, gathered the pieces of vase into a sheet of newspaper and slipped outside to put them in the garbage can. When my mother came into the living room, she spotted the smears on the hearth, glanced up at the mantel and asked, "Where's the little vase?"

I hung my head. "I dunno."

"Cynthia. Look at me." I had trouble meeting her gaze. "Did you break it?" she asked.

"No," I said, looking away from her dark blue eyes.

"Listen to me," my mother said. "If you broke it, you can tell me. If you tell me the truth, I'll never be angry with you. But if you lie, that makes me really cross. Did you break it?"

I burst into tears and confessed. She hugged me and told me that being honest and telling the truth were more important to her than any old vase.

When we'd had Joey for just four months, we came home one day to find him lying dead at the bottom of his cage. My mother looked stricken. "I'm sorry," Cynthia," she said. "I couldn't get his usual birdseed. The shopkeeper said the new brand was just as good but the seeds looked much bigger than the ones in his regular food. He must have choked to death." She was sad, for she'd grown fond of the little bird. We found a shoebox and we both cried as we buried him in the backyard.

A couple of months later, while Mum was broiling herrings for our supper, we heard mewing outside. I opened the door and let in a skinny little white cat with yellow eyes. We gave her a saucer of milk and a small plate of our leftover fish skin and bones. Later that evening, as we played Monopoly at the kitchen table, she curled up on my lap and purred herself to sleep. She had obviously decided to live with us. We called her Snowy. Every evening I pulled the cat onto my lap as we sat in front of our crackly radio listening to the six o'clock news.

By the end of 1941, the broadcasts told us there was a lull in the air raids, and my mother decided it was safe enough for us to visit Bubbe in north London for a week.

I helped pack our big suitcase. When we were ready to leave, Mum picked up Snowy and carried her out of the front door.

"Is she coming with us?" I asked, excited at the thought of introducing her to my grandmother, aunts and uncle.

"Don't dawdle, Cynthia," my mother said, putting Snowy down. "We'll miss the train."

We set off with Snowy trotting behind us. There was a major road at the end of our little street. Army convoys regularly drove along it, taking 20 minutes or more to pass.

"Should I carry Snowy?" I asked.

"No dear. She'll be fine."

We all made it across. On the other side of the main road, a footpath led toward the village, then divided near the railroad station. One path continued straight into the village, and a less well-trodden one veered right and went uphill to the station.

"Come on, puss, puss," I called to Snowy as we headed uphill.

But my mother picked up Snowy again and took her a few steps on the path leading to the village.

"Shoo. Shoo," she said, throwing the cat down rather roughly.

"What are you doing, Mummy? Isn't she coming with us?"

"Don't be ridiculous, Cynthia. She'll find another home just like she found us."

Mum's mouth was set in a hard line as she grabbed my hand and started to pull me up the hill towards the station. Below us, the little white cat trotted confidently toward the village. I began to cry and tried to pull away, but my mother kept a firm grip on my hand.

When we got into the train, I pressed my forehead against the window sobbing until I had no more tears and we rode on in silence. I couldn't look out at the scenery because the windows were painted black as part of the blackout protocols so I closed my eyes, exhausted from crying. Mummy put her arm around me, wiped my eyes, and helped me blow my nose. Then she gave me a little box of raisins, a special treat reserved for train rides like this one, and pulled a couple of comic magazines from her purse. I occupied myself with *Beano* and *Chicks' Own* for the rest of the journey.

At Bubbe's house, Uncle Goody smiled indulgently when I tried to contribute to the adult conversation, and Aunties Rose and Fan showered me with gifts: crayons, coloring books and a paint box. Auntie Milly was married now. She and her husband, my new Uncle Jack, came to visit one evening, and she gave me a beautiful Fair Isle cardigan she had knitted. Bubbe made special custard and semolina and served them to me in my favorite mug. There were no air raids or wailing sirens.

At the end of the week, we went back to South Godstone. I missed Snowy and shed tears when I remembered how brave she'd looked trotting down the path to the village.

Cynthia Ehrenkrantz

War Photos

An Anderson shelter, named after Sir John Anderson, the Minister of Home Security. My father built our Anderson shelter in the backyard of our Croydon house.

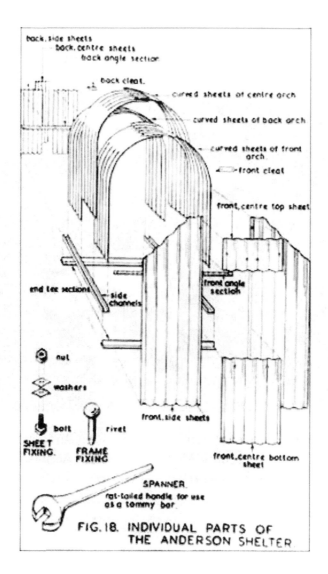

FIG. 18. INDIVIDUAL PARTS OF
THE ANDERSON SHELTER.

Anderson shelter building plan. My father
used this plan to install our backyard shelter.

A V1 Flying bomb. "Hitler's secret weapon." We called them "buzz bombs" because of their distinctive ear-splitting roar. They bombarded Southern England from June to October 1944.
More than 1,300 of these bombs fell on Croydon, my hometown.

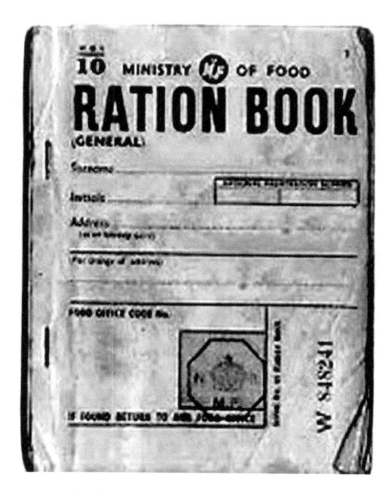

Ration books like this one were issued to everyone in
Britain starting in January, 1940

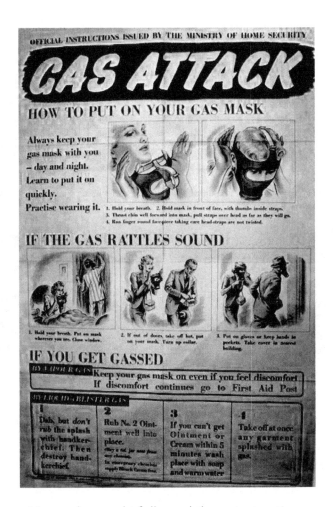

My mother and I followed these instructions
when we first tried on our gas masks.

My mother and I slept in a Morrison shelter like this one during the flying bomb attacks in 1944. Constructed like a big, cast iron table, it was slightly larger than a double bed and less than three feet high, but strong enough to bear the weight of a collapsed building so that survivors could be rescued

Unmanned barrage balloons like this one floated in the sky, ready to ensnare enemy airplanes in the steel cables that hung from them.

Cynthia Ehrenkrantz

PART FOUR:
KEEP CALM....

Chapter 18
Passover

I n March 1942, the RAF bombed the German port and medieval town of Lübeck, the first German city to be heavily damaged in an RAF attack. The next month, Germany launched retaliatory raids against a number of British historical and cultural centers, including Exeter, Bath, Norwich and Canterbury. These raids became known as the Baedeker Raids after a German spokesman said, "We shall go out and bomb every building in Britain marked with three stars in the Baedeker Guide," a popular British travel guide at the time. The raids received little news coverage because the government didn't want Germany to know if these attacks were successful. London was not a target so the skies back home remained quiet, and my parents were under the impression there had been a lull in hostilities.

My mother and I took the train to London Bridge Station again in early April 1942. The train's windows were still painted over, so I brought my copies of *Alice's Adventures in Wonderland* and *Through the Looking Glass* with me to read during the trip. But I was almost too excited to read because the evening ahead of us was the most special night of the year: Seder night, the first night of Passover.

As we made our way across London on underground trains and buses, Mummy told me that Bubbe had started planning for Passover a month before, right after the holiday of Purim. From then until Passover, lunch was often a hearty bowl of potato soup, and fish replaced the weekend chicken so she could put everyone's ration coupons aside for special Passover supplies. Extra pennies and shillings were saved in the biscuit barrel on the sideboard, for she needed lots of eggs and expensive ground almonds to go into gefillte fish, matzo balls and the delicious pancakes she made for breakfast during the eight-day holiday. Mummy was bringing a dozen eggs laid by our hens, carefully packed into an egg box she'd borrowed from a neighbor.

When we finally reached Bubbe's house, I ran down the tiled hallway toward the sound of "chink, chink, chink" coming from the scullery where Auntie Rose was making *charoset* – the sweet pasty mixture of apples, cinnamon, nuts and wine that we eat at the Seder to remind us of the mortar our slave-ancestors used when building monuments for the Egyptians. She was chopping and mixing the ingredients on a small plate: a dozen walnuts, an apple, cinnamon and a tablespoon or so of sweet wine. Nine eggs simmered gently on the stove.

The table was already set with chased silverware and gold-rimmed dishes Bubbe only used during Passover week. If someone gave her a beautiful dish or a pitcher, she always "saved it for Pesach," putting it aside on the top shelf of the larder. Her grown-up children made fun of her.

"All the best things are only used for eight days. That makes no sense, Ma."

But Bubbe ignored them, for at Pesach she believed we should all feel like royalty. Only the finest china, silver and crystal were good enough.

In the scullery, Auntie Rose set me to work peeling hard-boiled eggs. We kept the shell on one that she singed in a gas flame. It would go on the seder plate to remind us, she said, "of the destruction of the Temple." I'd never heard a synagogue called a temple. I only knew that a temple was

the side part of a person's forehead and I wondered whose
temple she was talking about and if their whole head had
been destroyed too.

I helped set up the seder plate with the burnt egg; a
lamb shank bone to remind us of the ancient paschal lamb
sacrifice; grated horseradish root to represent the bitterness
of slavery; parsley as a symbol of Spring, hope and renewal;
and a little bowl of salt water to represent the Israelite slaves'
tears. Now we were ready to start. The dining table was
normally pushed up against the wall but it had been pulled
away to make room for more people. Uncle Goody sat at the
head of the table, propped up on pillows. Auntie Fan told
me this was supposed to make him feel like a king on a
throne. Bubbe sat opposite him. My Aunties Rose, Fan and
Milly sat on the outside of the table so they could get up
easily to help Bubbe serve. Milly's husband, Jack, sat on the
inside with my mother and me. Daddy couldn't join us
because he was on duty at the fire station.

Uncle Goody led the Seder, gabbling through the
Haggadah and the story of the Jewish people's escape from
Egypt. It was all in Hebrew and he mumbled through the
text and prayers in a low monotone. I waited eagerly for my
turn, when I got to ask the four questions. I read them
slowly, sounding out the Hebrew letters as my mother had
taught me. *"Ma nishtana ha'layloh hazeh mikol ha'laylos?" Why
is this night different from all other nights?* Everyone around
the table nodded and smiled, and I felt like a princess.

We sang no songs, but we all joined in the blessings over
the special foods. I relished each one: the parsley sprig
freshly picked from Bubbe's garden, which we dipped in salt
water to remind us of the Sea of Reeds the Israelites had to
cross during the exodus from Egypt. Then there was the
wonderful spicy-sweet charoset, a teaspoonful on a little

piece of matzo, followed by the searing nibble of horseradish. It made my eyes water. Bubbe told us she had at last found a good use for her gas mask. She'd worn it while grating horseradish and it had worked like a charm. She hadn't shed one tear.

The real meal began with a strange, salty soup: a peeled, hard-boiled egg in a large bowl of salt water. My mother helped me slice the egg so it didn't splash on the lace tablecloth. Every year, Auntie Rose said, "If we were to eat this on any other day, we would hate it. But on this night, it's delicious."

Next came gefillte fish, each ball crowned with a thin slice of carrot. Bubbe brought these to the table on a huge oval platter decorated with a beautiful painted border of blue flowers. On this special night, she'd made *gedempte fleisch* for our main course: thin slices of garlicky pot roast served with crispy roast potatoes: one potato each for me, my mother, Bubbe and each of my aunts; two for Uncle Jack; three or four for Uncle Goody. Dessert was a compote of stewed prunes and apple rings.

Before the meal, Uncle Goody had given me a present: a Children's Haggadah with pictures that moved when you pulled a tab. I could watch Baby Moses floating in the bulrushes and I could drown the wicked Egyptian army in the Sea of Reeds. There was even a picture of a boy finding the *afikoman*, the piece of matzo his father had hidden just as Uncle Goody had hidden one for me. I looked for it while the grownups drank lemon tea from glasses inserted into brass holders. When I found it tucked behind one of Uncle Goody's bed pillows, he gave me another gift as my prize: a book token to spend at the local book store.

My mother and I shared Auntie Rose's bed with her that night, nestled like three spoons. In the morning, after a breakfast of Bubbe's delicious almond pancakes, Mummy and I made the long trip back to South Godstone, where fields of wild flowers reminded us in another way that it was springtime.

Cynthia Ehrenkrantz

Chapter 19
Homecoming

In July 1942, Mummy told me we were going to leave South Godstone and go back to Croydon. Daddy had a three-day leave and came down to help us pack, and Mummy sang as she did housework. I started to get really excited at the thought of returning to our very own house. When we lugged our suitcases to South Godstone station, it was hard to believe we were finally leaving the countryside and going home to Croydon.

Back in our flat, my mother's joy at being in her own home was palpable. No day in South Godstone had passed without her complaining about the boredom of living in the country and how much she missed shops, theater and cinemas. Her happiness at having returned to Croydon was infectious. This was going to be a happy time. My parents were back together at last and I could enjoy my own books and toys.

In my old bedroom, I bounced on the bed and for the first time in my life cried tears of joy. At last, I would sleep in my own bed, not share one with my mother while she complained about my constant fidgeting. I sat in the wicker armchair Auntie Rose had given me. I pulled out the drawers of my very own bureau, painted pale green to match the window frames and baseboard. Then I looked up at the picture on the wall: a boy and his dog. It was nighttime and the boy was sitting on a fallen log in the middle of a moonlit forest. He held a flashlight and his dog sat next to him, her head on his knee, gazing up at her young master. It was clear that he'd been lost and the heroic dog had found him.

I ran downstairs to the kitchen where my parents were drinking tea.

"When are we going to get Judy?" I asked. "Does Mrs. Chapman live far away? Can we go today?"

My parents looked at each other across the kitchen table as I danced from one foot to the other. My mother turned to me. Her eyes were very bright and her nose was red.

"Cynthia darling," she said. "Judy isn't at Mrs. Chapman's. We had to put her to sleep when we moved to the country."

"Put her to sleep? Put her to sleep?" I was screaming now. "How could you do that? You told me she'd come home with us at the end of the bombing."

"We had to do it, darling," my mother said. "Food was rationed, and we didn't know how we could feed her. Everyone was putting their pets to sleep. And, besides, she was old and smelly. No one would have wanted her."

"But *I* want her," I sobbed. "Old and smelly? I loved her smell. *I* want her. You lied to me! You lied! For two whole years you lied. I hate you! I *hate* you!"

I ran upstairs, slammed the door to my room and threw myself face down on my bed. Tears soaked my cheeks, the salt stinging my skin. My mother was always going on about honesty and truth being the most important things in the world to her, but Judy, my Judy, was gone forever and my mother had lied about her over and over. I swore I would never forgive her.

I turned over, looked at the picture of the boy with his dog and wailed at the moon in the picture.

Chapter 20
Croydon High

Although the war continued to rage in Europe, North Africa and the Pacific, and bombs were falling on other parts of Britain, London was calm in the summer of 1942. As soon as my mother and I moved back to Croydon, she arranged for me to take the entrance exam for Croydon High School for Girls, the finest private school in our London suburb.

My parents had no ambition for me to go to college. Higher education was not part of their world. But they were both determined to give me the best education they could afford. My mother especially hoped I would come out of Croydon High speaking with an upper-class accent, which she saw as a passport to a better life and the possibility of marrying well. As soon as we returned to Croydon, she started working as an invoice clerk for Ellis and Goldstein, a clothing manufacturer in London's East End. Her salary, she said, would cover my school fees.

Most Croydon High School girls entered in kindergarten and stayed till they were 18, going on to university and professions. But the war had disrupted that routine as girls had been evacuated to the country, making more spaces available for older incoming students like me.

I was nervous about the entrance exam because my arithmetic was so poor. My mother drilled me on the multiplication tables and I tried really hard to learn them because I sensed this new school was something to strive for.

On a warm July day, sun streamed in through the windows of a classroom where I sat with about 20 other girls reading a poem. When we finished, we were told to write down our thoughts about what the poet was trying to say. I had lots of ideas and wrote my answer as fast as I could. Next came arithmetic. The drills helped. I was able to answer most of the problems, but not all of them. After we completed the English and arithmetic exams, we waited in line outside an office and were called in one by one to meet the headmistress, Miss Adams, a plump Scotswoman with piercing blue eyes and pale red hair. She asked me where I'd gone to school up to then, what my favorite subject was and what I liked to read.

After the interviews were completed, we were ushered out onto the playground. A girl wearing her hair in one long blond braid was skillfully shooting baskets on the netball court and invited me to play. I was no athlete and could barely hit the rim of the basket, but she cheerfully passed me the ball every time she scored. She told me her name was Jayne Dale and I should remember to spell Jayne with a "y."

"What did Miss Adams ask you?" I inquired.

"She asked me what I liked to read and I said comics," Jayne said.

I had discussed *Alice in Wonderland*. I'd read it so many times, I had it just about memorized. I hoped Jayne had passed the exam. She seemed nice, and if we both passed I thought we'd be friends.

The following week, a letter came saying I'd been accepted into Croydon High School.

"Wonderful news," my mother said. "I didn't think you'd pass because your arithmetic is so terrible. They must be really short of pupils if they let you in."

The acceptance letter included strict instructions about uniform requirements, the guidelines paying little regard to the fact that clothes were rationed.

"We'll have to use some of Daddy's clothing coupons," my mother said. "It's a good thing he wears a fireman's uniform so he can spare them."

On a bright sunny morning six weeks later, I stood in my mother's bedroom admiring myself in her full-length mirror. It was September 7, 1942. I was nine, it was the first day of school, and I was proud to be wearing my new school uniform: a V-necked, navy blue jumper that we called a gym tunic over a sparkling white, long sleeved blouse, with a dark green tie neatly knotted under the collar. The long leather strap of a change purse crossed from my right shoulder to my left hip. White ankle socks and shiny brown shoes completed my outfit. I put on my brand new navy blue overcoat—I'd outgrown my old one—and my new black velour hat with its white hatband and green enameled ivy leaf badge pinned to the front and pirouetted in front of the mirror. I thought I looked splendid.

Walking to school on that first day, my mother and I passed a two-year-old bomb site on Lower Addiscombe Road. Rubble had been cleared away and stalks of delicate pink flowers we called London Pride were poking their way up through cracks in the building's foundation. As we drew near the school I let go of my mother's hand and joined a crowd of girls all wearing uniforms exactly like mine. Each girl carried a red cloth drawstring bag with her name embroidered in green on the outside. The bags held one pair of house shoes to change into as soon as we arrived in the morning and a pair of sneakers we called plimsolls for gym and sports. As we streamed in through the entrance, I thought we looked like a girls' army, all dressed alike. I was glad to meet Jayne in the cloakroom where we hung our coats, hats and shoe bags. She was the only person I knew in the milling crowd of girls.

We changed into our house shoes, and a group of older girls directed us to our classrooms. They wore skirts instead of jumpers and had a single silver bar attached to their green ties. I found out later they were prefects – privileged sixth formers who shouldered many responsibilities. One of them directed me down a wide hallway with a shiny, newly waxed floor.

As I entered the classroom, a teacher stopped me at the door.

"We don't wear shoes like that in Croydon High School," she said, pointing down at my feet. When my mother and I had packed my red cloth bag the night before, we had discovered that I'd outgrown my only other pair of shoes and she had cut away the leather over my toes so I could still wear them as house shoes at school. Posters and advertisements were telling us to *Make Do and Mend,* and she'd seen this suggestion in a pamphlet. I felt the color rise in my cheeks and hung my head. We'd spent so much time and money and so many clothing coupons on my uniform and we still hadn't got it right. The following weekend, my mother borrowed coupons from one of her sisters and bought me new shoes.

Our homeroom teacher, Miss Mounsey, was a middle-aged woman with a quivery voice and graying hair scraped back into a bun. She wore a long string of beads that she played with absentmindedly.

The day began with Miss Mounsey telling us about Croydon High School's standards of behavior.

"High School girls conduct themselves with dignity when they are outside the school," she said. "Everyone in Croydon recognizes your uniform and you represent the school wherever you go."

How different this was from Godstone Station School where I'd been told that wearing my old school uniform was "putting on airs." At last, I was in a place where there were lots of other girls who dressed just like me.

"You must speak quietly to one another when you're on the street," Miss Mounsey continued. "No loud laughing or wild behavior. And *always* give up your seat on the bus to older people. When you're inside the school, there is to be no running in the corridors. Walk in single file and keep to the left. You will stand up whenever a teacher enters the room or when you're called on in class."

The next day, we elected a class captain and vice-captain by secret ballot. These girls would have to keep order when a teacher left the room and would have other responsibilities, like collecting papers at the end of a lesson. The only girl I knew was Jayne so I voted for her. Secret ballots? Democratic elections? I'd never experienced such activities before.

Our classroom was bright and airy. Reproductions of the works of Old Masters hung on the walls and fresh flower arrangements stood on the windowsill, changed every week by the girl who was appointed "flower monitor." Our desks weren't pitted and scratched like the ones in South Godstone and we were taught in a way that I found almost seductive.

The first book we read was *Theras: The Story of an Athenian Boy* by Caroline Dale Snedeker. After we read it, we turned it into a play and were all assigned parts. Jayne played the part of Theras and I was his pedagogue, his personal slave. I threw myself into the joy of acting, adopting a dignified manner as I watched over my young master. It was thrilling to imagine living in ancient Greece and pretending to believe in mythical gods and goddesses.

The other girls admired my uninhibited performance. They were stiff and much shyer than I was.

We were preparing to perform the play in front of our parents and several other classes, so Miss Mounsey gave out costumes. Mine was a dusty pink shapeless twill garment that hung on me like a sack. Miss Mounsey told me to secure it with a belt from home.

I took the robe home and paraded in front of my mother.

"It looks terrible, Cynthia," she said. "It's three sizes too big for you. A belt isn't going to help." And, indeed, it was so big, the bodice was almost falling off me, showing most of my undershirt.

Seeing me perform on stage was very important to my mother, and she wanted me to look my best. The next day, she left work early and came in to school to ask Miss Mounsey if I could have a different costume.

"I'm afraid not," Miss Mounsey said, looking annoyed. "That's the only costume available. She'll have to make do with it."

Even though she had trained as a milliner, my mother hated sewing and regarded working with her hands as demeaning. But she overcame her aversion, cobbling the robe together as best she could, securing the shoulders to my undershirt with safety pins. When we performed the play, the belt bunched around my skinny waist and the robe still kept slipping off my shoulders. I adopted a magisterial stance grasping the front of my dress with one hand and gesticulating with the other. I could see Mummy in the back row, wagging her head from side to side in disapproval. I knew she was thinking how awful I looked in that dreadful robe. But when we took our bows, I received more applause than anyone else and I stopped caring about the ugly costume.

Theras paved the way for Thomas Bulfinch's *The Age of Fable,* and Greek myths became as familiar as nursery rhymes. Later, when we read poems or plays that mentioned those ancient deities, we understood the references straight away.

Nature study introduced us to the birds, trees and flowers surrounding us. We drew pictures of them, learned scientific names for the parts of a flower and observed the behavior of black-headed gulls swooping down for their prey on the school playing field.

There were sports activities every day: rounders (a kind of softball), hockey and netball. And on days when we didn't have sports outdoors we exercised in the gym, where we climbed ropes and leapt over "horses."

The war was a great leveler. Almost every girl's father was doing National Service like my dad. But in civilian life, the other girls' fathers were professional men: doctors, lawyers, bankers. My father, on the other hand, was a shopkeeper, which was termed "in trade." After the war, he would go back to owning a store. I imagined my friends' parents becoming his customers. He'd have to wait on them, almost like a servant in a grand house. The thought made me uncomfortable.

Diana, one of my new friends, invited me to her birthday party. Her three-story house was surrounded by neatly clipped lawns with herbaceous borders in full bloom. I lived in an upstairs apartment in a house where chickens clucked at the end of our yard. That day, I realized I was not as privileged as my new friends.

In other ways, though, I felt more entitled than they were. An only child, doted on by my parents, aunts, uncle and grandmother, I was accustomed to being the center of attention, and it was hard to give that up.

"I know! I know!" I would shout out in class, waving my arm frantically, begging to be called on. But Miss Mounsey ignored me most of the time or only glared in my direction. I felt she didn't like me.

One day, she was giving a spelling test and I didn't hear one of the words. Instead of raising my hand as I was supposed to do, I said out loud, "Would you please repeat that?" and for Miss Mounsey this was the last straw. Her eyes narrowed and she scowled at me.

"Cynthia Shelower, put down your pen. The rest of you will carry on."

I did as instructed. Tears stung my eyes as I realized she'd stopped me from continuing with the test. I'd never failed an English test in my life. I teared up again as I told my mother about the injustice, and she marched into school with me the next morning—the second time she had complained to Miss Mounsey. Confronting a teacher, expressing displeasure—such behavior on the part of a parent was unheard of in Croydon High School, where students learned about the virtues of the stiff upper lip. They took their punishments without complaint and were supposed to learn from them. Parents didn't come to school unless they were invited for a parents' meeting or a concert. My mother was an expert complainer but her efforts didn't help me one bit. They only made Miss Mounsey dislike me more.

One of the girls disliked me, too, for a different reason. Isabel Jones approached me on the playground one day with a group of her friends.

"My mummy says we're in this war because of Jews like you," she said. "Why don't you go back to your own country?"

"This *is* my country," I protested. "I was born here and so were my parents."

"No, you weren't," she said. "You're lying. You're a foreigner. A Jew." She stuck her tongue out, turned around and flounced away with her friends, leaving me standing bewildered and alone in a corner of the playground. She hadn't hit me or felt for horns on my head like the boys in South Godstone, but this kind of hurt was just as bad. I felt my stomach tighten and bit my lip to keep from crying.

Just seven Jewish girls including myself attended Croydon High along with about 400 Christian girls who filed in to prayers every morning. While the rest of the students gathered in the assembly hall and sat cross-legged on the floor to sing hymns and read from *The Book of Common Prayer*, we Jewish girls conducted our own prayers in one of the classrooms. A senior girl read a prayer in Hebrew and we took turns reading one of the psalms in English. The sound of 400 girls reciting The Lord's Prayer in the big hall was our signal to line up single file outside the hall and march in. Each morning we filed past rows of girls sitting on the floor and teachers seated in chairs against the wall to our assigned places at the front of the hall, where we sat one behind the other and listened to the day's announcements. Every morning, hundreds of heads turned as we entered and hundreds of pairs of eyes stared as we made our march. Often, Miss Needham, one of the teachers, would lean forward as I passed and whisper, "Pull your shoulders back, Cynthia. Stand up straight."

I didn't understand why we had to enter in such a conspicuous way. I wondered why we couldn't slip in quietly and sit at the back of the hall. That daily walk down to the front seemed intended to emphasize that we were different from the other girls. I cringed inside every time we had to do it, but I said nothing to my mother. I was learning how to be a proper Croydon High School student.

In South Godstone, I'd been teased and bullied for being different—for being Jewish and middle class and living in a town instead of being Christian, working class and raised on a farm. Croydon High School girls, for the most part, were too well brought up to bully people physically or verbally. I made friends, but I was aware of a chasm between us. A chasm of class and religion. Even though we all wore the same uniform and looked alike, I still felt like an outsider looking in.

Cynthia Ehrenkrantz

Chapter 21
The Kitchen Front

By 1943, the war seemed far away from us in Croydon. We followed the news reports about battles in North Africa, where my Uncle Victor's son Shullum was posted. His letters home spoke of dysentery, flies and unbearable heat.

We performed air-raid drills regularly at school, filing into concrete-lined rooms where we carried on with our lessons in a business-as-usual mode. But actual nighttime air raids had just about ceased.

On September 8, 1943, when I was 10, it was announced that Italy had surrendered to the Allies. Miss Adams called for a school assembly where we gave three cheers in the traditional fashion: she called out "Hip hip," and we all yelled "Hurray!" in joyful unison.

But the fighting continued, in Italy and other parts of the world, and at home we all still struggled to get by and do our bit for the war effort. We were urged to conserve fuel by filling the bathtub with only five inches of warm water. The King, we were told, bathed in five inches just as we did. When I spent time in Uncle Goody's tailor shop, one of my jobs was to cut newspaper into neat squares, poke holes in the corners and thread the pieces onto a string loop that we hung in the toilet to be used as toilet paper.

Canned goods were rationed through a complex system of points, and the only bread available was the National Loaf, a heavy, dense, dirty beige whole wheat bread that everyone complained about. People were sure it was fortified with sawdust instead of vitamins and calcium. We longed for the white bread we'd eaten before the war but were told the National Loaf was a necessity because it used every part of the wheat except the stalks and was far more nutritious. Bread-slicing machines had been banned as a waste of energy, and bread was not sold until 12 hours after it was baked. Freshly baked bread is harder to slice thinly and it's so tasty, people eat more of it. While the wheatmeal loaf was regarded as nasty, dirty, coarse, dark and indigestible, it was better than nothing.

We were constantly being urged not to waste food. Posters and billboards reminded us that *A clear plate means a clear conscience,* and once a week, on the Wednesday morning broadcast of *The Kitchen Front,* The Radio Doctor, later revealed to be Dr. Charles Hill, gave us chatty information about nutrition. From him I learned about protein, carbohydrates and vitamins, and it was Dr. Hill who taught us not to peel vegetables but to scrub them clean or scrape them very lightly because the skin contained valuable nutrients.

Candy was now also rationed and I was given my own coupons to spend as I liked. Chocolate melted in the mouth too quickly, so I often chose hard candies because they lasted a long time. Before the war, I had loved eating Jelly Babies and pretending to be a little cannibal, biting off the head, arms and legs before popping the body in my mouth. But there were none to be had during the war. We all bought gobstoppers, huge balls of hard candy that we could barely fit into our mouths. As they dissolved, they changed color, and we would pop them out every few minutes to monitor their progress. I loved Sherbet Fountain, a sweet flavored powder in a little paper tube fitted with a licorice straw. It fizzed in my mouth and caused much coughing as some of it inevitably went down the wrong way and exploded in my throat.

By the time we moved back to Croydon, an official British Restaurant had opened at the end of our road. Originally established to help feed people who'd been bombed out of their homes or had run out of rations, British Restaurants were government-funded, locally run canteens where anyone could get a three-course meal for a maximum of nine pence, about $2.50 today, and dessert and tea for a few pence more. My mother often told me to eat lunch there when she was working and I had a half day of school.

I found the food almost inedible and struggled to get it down. Mince was ground meat of dubious origin served plain-boiled without the help of onions or garlic. Greasy, gristly and hard to chew, it lay on the plate in a pale-beige puddle, usually accompanied by watery potatoes and dark green, bitter cabbage – all boiled for a very long time. (We were urged not to discard the dark green outer leaves of cabbage because they were very nutritious.) Dessert was often stewed apples and custard. The apples were peeled but not cored and harbored little toe-nail-clipping-like pieces of seeds and pulp; I would discreetly spit them into my hand to line up on the edge of the plate. Bird's Custard Powder—an eggless mixture of cornflour, flavoring and food coloring—was a staple of every British larder. My mother and grandmother mixed it with milk so it was like a runny vanilla pudding. British Restaurant custard was made with water and often contained little slimy lumps of powder that congealed on my stewed apples, forming an unappetizing skin on top. I learned to say, "No custard, please."

The United States was now sending us bottles of concentrated orange juice, which were provided free for children under age five and pregnant and nursing women. A teaspoonful in a glass of water made a weak-flavored orangeade. America was also supplying us with cod liver oil

—nauseatingly greasy and reeking of old fish—which was also distributed free to the same populations. Thanks to the Americans, we now also had powdered eggs, which were useful when added to recipes but had a grayish color and pasty consistency when scrambled.

Citrus was still a rarity. My mother and I were walking in London's West End one day when a convoy of American servicemen was passing through. A soldier sitting in the back of a truck was peeling an orange. I pointed at him and said, "Look, Mummy! An orange!"

"Don't point," my mother said. "It's rude."

The soldier heard me, reached into his pack and threw an orange down to me, but I fumbled it and it bounced along in the gutter. We chased it down the street, picked it up and took it home. Mummy washed off the dirt, peeled it for me and looked on smiling while I carefully separated the sections and ate each one very slowly, relishing every squirt of juice.

I was invited to a birthday party just after a rare shipment of lemons had appeared in the stores. My schoolmate's mother took full advantage of the luxury and served lemon curd sandwiches, lemon cake with lemon frosting, and a lemon mousse. It was all delicious, but I spent the night throwing up, my stomach rebelling at the over-abundance of the strange, sour fruit.

Chapter 22
Doodlebugs

We began seeing more and more American and Canadian soldiers in the streets as the months went by. Daddy suspected something big was about to happen.

On June 6, 1944, when I was 11, we sat glued to the radio as we listened to reports of the Allied invasion of Normandy —D-Day. My parents sat pressed close together, tightly clasping each other's hands. Perhaps the end of the war was in sight.

We tuned in to the news every evening, our hopes rising with each report that Allied troops were gaining ground. But only a week later, in the early morning of June 13, Hitler launched his Secret Weapon: the V-1 missile. The first one fell on Bethnal Green in London's East End and was followed by days and nights of almost nonstop bombing. We were once more thrust into the terror of war from the air.

The experience of V-1s raining down on London was far more terrifying than the Luftwaffe air raids we'd experienced during the Blitz. Luftwaffe pilots had dropped bombs from airplanes aiming for specific targets, but V-1s had no pilots so they seemed particularly sinister. They were launched across the channel from German-controlled parts of the French and Dutch coasts: huge, autopiloted flying bombs. Without the technology for precision strikes, they fell almost randomly within a rough target area—on open ground, houses, schools, factories and theaters. We called them buzz bombs or Doodlebugs because they made a distinctive buzzing sound as they approached, a bit like a very loud motorcycle as it came nearer and nearer.

As long as we heard the sound, we knew we were safe. Then, when a Doodlebug started its dive, the rattling buzz stopped and there was silence. Sometimes, the bomb hit within a few seconds; at other times, we would wait for almost a minute while it seemed to float overhead. The silence was followed by an earsplitting explosion when the bomb crashed to earth. Each Doodlebug carried just under a ton of high explosives. The blast destroyed everything for hundreds of yards around. Solid walls crumbled, individual bricks in a wall were reduced to pebble-sized bits. Windows a quarter of a mile away cracked from the force of the explosion.

During the Blitz, nearly all the air raids had happened at night. But Doodlebugs flew over us around the clock, causing terror and devastation as they rained mostly over the south of England. From June to the middle of September 1944, 162 Doodlebugs landed on Croydon, destroying more than 1,000 buildings and damaging more than 57,000 others. Over 200 people were killed and nearly 2,000 were injured. When the air-raid sirens wailed, my stomach dropped like lead and I had to run to the bathroom quickly to avoid messing in my pants. Sitting on the toilet with my eyes screwed tightly shut, I would try to breathe deeply to calm my fear before running to the shelter.

Ever since we'd returned from South Godstone in the summer of 1942, we'd been sleeping in our own beds in our upstairs apartment. When the Doodlebug campaign began, we started sleeping in the downstairs flat now occupied by our new tenants, Mr. and Mrs. Borton, sharing a Morrison shelter that had replaced the backyard Anderson. Outdoor Anderson shelters had proved unpopular because they were so ill-suited to the damp English climate. The Morrison shelter was a large, steel, table-high, rectangular cage with a solid top panel and a hefty frame that screwed together with chunky nuts and bolts. A grid of heavy wires stretched across the bottom as a mattress support and the mesh side panels could be opened from the inside for easy escape. It was sturdy enough to withstand the weight of a collapsed building and could be used as a dining table when the mesh side panels were removed.

Mr. Borton was a dapper little man who worked in London as a master tailor. He was skinny and short and wore rimless glasses perched on the end of his beaky nose. Mrs. Borton was a compulsive housekeeper who kept a stockpot simmering on her stove, sending nauseating smells of cooked cabbage, bacon rinds and turnips up to our apartment. She had a big bosom and a matching protuberant behind.

The Morrison shelter was slightly larger than a double bed, so we had to lie crosswise on the mattress and the grownups had to bend their knees to fit in. My father was almost always on night duty at the fire station, but on the rare nights he slept at home, he stayed upstairs in our flat, which made my mother extremely anxious. Mr. Borton slept at one end of the Morrison, Mrs. Borton was next to him, and I lay wriggling and fidgeting next to her. My mother was on my other side, squished in at the other end. Mrs. Borton made sure that she was as far away from Mr. Borton as possible. Later, my mother would laugh about Mrs. Borton's enforced sleeping order.

"He's so old, little and wrinkled," she'd say. Mr. Borton was probably in his early fifties.

My father would come home from the night shift exhausted, collapse into bed and fall into a deep sleep. Being careful not to disturb him, my mother and I tiptoed around the house, whispering to one another as we got dressed and ate breakfast. Then she would walk me to school, kiss me goodbye, say, "Have a wonderful day, darling," and walk two more blocks to West Croydon station to catch the train to London Bridge. From there, she rode the underground to her clerical job in the East End of London.

On the morning of June 29, my mother and I were walking to school together and had almost reached the school when we heard the unmistakable buzzing rattle of a Doodlebug, which I spotted in the distant sky. Then the noise stopped, followed by the diabolical silence. As it started to descend, the bomb looked as if it were directly overhead. Glancing upward, my mother pushed me to the ground and threw herself on top of me.

The rocket exploded about 100 yards away. Glass shattered out of hundreds of windows. The ground shook under us and several nearby buildings collapsed, crashing down with a deafening din. My mother and I lay there together. At first, I thought she must have died, her weight was so heavy on top of me. But then she started to tremble uncontrollably and I heaved a sigh of relief as I realized she was still alive. We waited for the noise of crumbling bricks and tinkling glass to stop. At last, when all was quiet, we staggered to our feet, shaking, and brushed the dirt off our grazed hands and knees. Dust was swirling all around making us cough. My knees felt as if they were melting as we walked the last few yards into the school building. A white-faced teacher stood just inside the doorway, blood pouring down her forehead into her eyes. Girls were milling about, pale and weeping. In spite of the confused scene in front of us, I was afraid my mother might think that school, with its concrete-lined air-raid shelters, would be the safest place for me. I burst into tears, threw my arms around her waist and cried, "Don't leave me, Mummy! Don't leave me! Please, please take me with you!"

My mother, dazed herself, asked the teacher, "Would you like me to take Cynthia into work with me today?"

"I think that would be best," the teacher replied, her voice trembling.

My mother looked down at me. "Of course I won't leave you," she said. "We'll stay together today."

Although I was 11, I held tightly onto my mother's hand like a five-year-old as we walked to the station and caught the train. My legs felt as if they'd turned to water and I was afraid of falling.

At her office, my mother was very apologetic about having to bring me to work. In the Keep Calm and Carry On atmosphere of wartime London, bringing children to work was frowned upon. She found a place for me to sit in a cloakroom on a wooden bench. I pulled a book out of my school satchel and started to read, but when I got to the bottom of the page, I couldn't remember what I had read at the top. I lay down on the hard bench, spread my coat over me like a blanket and fell into a deep sleep. I couldn't remember any other time when I'd slept in the middle of the day.

That night, my mother folded me into her arms as I snuggled close to her in the Morrison shelter. When the air-raid siren wailed, I lay stiff, holding my breath, my eyes wide open, staring into the darkness as I listened for the rattling drone of Doodlebugs. I finally fell into a fitful sleep as dawn was breaking.

My school was temporarily closed. Windows had been blown out and ceilings had fallen, so I went to work with my mother for the next few days. My father wasn't home much as he was called out for extra duty, putting out fires and digging through rubble to rescue casualties and remove the dead.

Within a week, my parents decided to send me back to Grandpa's house in Wales.

PART FIVE:
"V" FOR VICTORY

Chapter 23
Return to Wales

I didn't cry when my mother left to return to Croydon the
morning after we arrived at Grandpa's house. Still, I felt
knots in my stomach when the door closed behind her.
The London area was so dangerous, with flying bombs
exploding every day. I closed my eyes tight shut and
muttered a little prayer: "Please keep them safe. Please keep
my parents safe."

The last time I'd stayed in Merthyr Tydfil had been at
the beginning of the war, in 1939, when I was six – almost a
baby, I told myself. Back then, Grandpa had mostly ignored
me and my Aunts Dolly and Nellie had been preoccupied
with taking care of Grandma and working in Grandpa's
shop. I had spent a lot of time alone and unhappy. Now I
was 11 and much more independent—almost grown up, I
reasoned—so I thought things would be very different this
time around. It was July and the days were long and balmy. I
hoped Auntie Dolly would let me explore the little town on
my own.

> Dear Mummy and Daddy,
> Auntie Dolly helped me unpack my suitcase
> after you left, Mummy.
> Thank you so much for the Cadbury's
> chocolate. I found it at the bottom of the case. It
> was a lovely surprise. I am sleeping in Auntie
> Nellie's bedroom so I have plenty of room to put

my things. There's a big dressing table, just like
yours, with a three-section mirror. It makes me
feel very grown-up.

I hope you are both keeping safe. Daddy,
don't fall off any ladders.

Lots of love,
Cynthia

I was sorry that my vivacious Auntie Nellie wasn't living in
the house anymore but I was happy to hear that she was
doing well. Auntie Dolly told me that Nellie had risen
quickly through the ranks in her job at the aircraft factory
and was now a supervisor.

My darling Cynthia,

Thank you for your letter. It arrived today.
Isn't the post office wonderful to keep getting our
letters delivered even though there's a war on?

I ordered a subscription to the Girl's Own
Paper *for you. I know you love that magazine.*
Are you helping Auntie Dolly around the house?
She has lots to do, taking care of Grandpa and
Sylvia, and managing the shop. Perhaps you can
play with Sylvia or give Auntie Dolly a hand in
the kitchen.

Daddy and I are both well. He has to work
extra shifts at the fire station right now so he's
not home very much. He sends his love and, of
course, so do I.

Lots of love,
Mummy

In 1944, my widowed Auntie Dolly was just as overworked as she'd been in 1939. Shopkeeping and housework still held no interest for her, but with Nellie gone, she now had to take care of her toddler daughter, Sylvia, keep house for Grandpa and help him manage the store. My presence just added to her workload. Rationing had become more stringent and she resented having to cook for another person. She barked commands at me and often lost her temper, then finally decided to make the best of a bad job and use me as a mother's helper. I had no love for domestic tasks or babysitting, either, and we were at loggerheads most of the time.

> *Dear Mummy and Daddy,*
> *Auntie Dolly asked me to take care of Sylvia when she went to the shop today. She is such a whiny little girl. Was I like that when I was two? I tried to make her behave but she's not very obedient.*
> *I don't think Auntie Dolly likes having me here. She nags me all the time to pick up my things and tidy up my room. If it's my room, why can't I keep it the way I want to?*
> *Thank you for the stamps. Auntie Dolly offered to post my letters but I'm afraid she'll open them and I only want you to read them.*
> *Lots of love,*
> *Cynthia*

A cloud of anger hung over the Merthyr house. Dolly disciplined little Sylvia by giving her sharp smacks on her bottom. When I babysat, I followed suit and Sylvia's wails echoed through the big Victorian house.

Auntie Dolly and Grandpa didn't have normal conversations. They just snapped at each other. At mealtimes, Dolly banged plates of bland and often burnt food on the table in front of her father and he ate noisily, smacking his lips and slurping his soup. He never said, "Thank you." He just grunted at her. On most evenings, he went out, slamming the door behind him. Once a week, a group of his cronies came to the house to play poker just as they had the last time I was there and the room filled with smoke and smelled of cigarettes, cigars and whiskey for days.

The only people I heard speaking in normal voices were radio announcers. Every evening, we turned on the crackly radio to hear "This is the BBC Home Service. Here is the six o'clock news and this is Alvar Liddell reading it." The BBC had decided that news announcers should give their names so we could be assured that this was real news and not something broadcast by the enemy, because there were enemy broadcasts. Many families listened to one particular program called *Germany Calling,* hosted by a pro-Nazi British subject named William Joyce who moved to Germany shortly before England declared war. People called him Lord Haw-Haw because of his affected upper-class accent. Everyone knew that most of what he spouted was German propaganda and that he lied and exaggerated Nazi victories. But his broadcasts also often contained nuggets of real information that the British media didn't share, including the names of ships that had been torpedoed and the identities of British casualities and fatalities. Some people also found him witty and enjoyed his denunciations of the British ruling class. There was an entertaining quality to his broadcasts that kept people listening.

Mostly, though, we tuned into to the BBC, and the voices of Mr. Liddell, Frank Philips and Stuart Hibberd became familiar to us as we listened to them read the news every evening. I had arrived in Merthyr in July 1944, a month after D-Day, and we followed the progress of the Allies as they advanced through France, Italy, Belgium and Holland. When the announcers reported bad news, their voices dropped several tones and they sounded extra serious and solemn as they reported, "Some of our aircraft are missing…" or "…a number of casualties, some fatal…." News reports were frustratingly vague. There were no weather reports, for they would have given vital information to the Germans about the conditions for launching flying bombs over England. Every day while I was in Merthyr we heard of "air raids in the South East." "The South East" meant Croydon to me and I chewed my nails as I worried about my parents' safety.

After the Home Service news, the bouncy tune "Lillibulero" would introduce the BBC World Service news, which often contained direct reports from the battlefield. The foreign correspondents described brutal scenes around them and the sounds of explosions and gunfire accompanied their commentaries.

When I'd stayed in Merthyr at the beginning of the war, it had been the depths of winter. Now it was summer and many days were bathed in watery sunshine. Grandpa's garden backed on to Penydarren Park, where coal miners exercised their whippets in the late afternoons, whistling commands at the dogs. The whippets looked like miniature greyhounds and their owners trained them to race one another. I watched them through a gap in the hedge and longed for a dog of my own.

Merthyr is a hilly town, and the garden was terraced up the hillside with stone steps going straight up the middle.

Gnarled apple trees were heavy with fruit, and blackcurrant, redcurrant and gooseberry bushes tumbled down the slope. One hot afternoon, Dolly gave me a big colander and told me to pick blackcurrants while she picked the red ones. The next day she said I could help her make jam. Sugar was rationed so we used bitter-tasting saccharine to sweeten our tea and saved sugar to make preserves. I helped Dolly strip blackcurrants off their stems with a fork and watched her boil fruit and sugar together in a big shallow pan. I loved the steamy, fruity smell and she let me test drops on a plate, pushing them with my finger till we were sure the jam had jelled. Then she began ladling it into glass jars she'd put aside all winter.

"Get out of the way," she said when I asked if I could help ladle the hot jam. "The last thing I need is for you to go home all scalded and scarred."

Bread and jam sandwiches were staples at teatime, and preserves made the gritty National Loaf more palatable.

On another occasion, we picked apples from the apple tree to store in the attic. We rubbed them with margarine and laid them out in rows on newspaper we'd put on the floor.

Mondays were laundry days, and Dolly poked and stirred the white clothes with a stick as they bubbled away in the huge copper boiler filled with water into which she had added a cube of Reckitt's Blue, which was supposed to make the clothes look extra white. I helped her put clothes through the wringer and hang them on the clothesline. When they were all secured with clothespins, she propped up the heavy line with a long, forked wooden pole. The clothes flapped in the breeze and dried quickly. Sometimes, of course, it rained and we had to rush out to take everything down from the line and rehang the laundry on wooden clothes horses in the house.

Dolly never offered to play checkers or board games with me like my parents did. Left to my own devices, I took refuge in reading, visiting the library several times a week. The children's department was very small so I graduated to the adult shelves and lost myself in the romance of James Hilton's *Lost Horizon* and the novels of Mazo de la Roche.

There were only a couple of weeks left in the school year when I arrived in Merthyr, so instead of insisting I attend the local school, my teachers from Croydon loaded me with homework assignments. I completed them conscientiously and mailed them back but it was lonely working all by myself in my bedroom with no friends around.

One evening, as Dolly, Grandpa, Sylvia and I were eating supper, I complained aloud that some of my math problems were really hard. I was hoping for a little sympathy but I got none. Dolly just kept eating and Grandpa turned to Sylvia. "Sylvia vill soon be able to help you mit dem," he said, not even looking at me. "She's such a clever gel. Aren't you, Sylvia?"

"Yeth, I am a clever girl," Sylvia lisped. I stared down at my plate with a lump in my throat.

Dear Mummy and Daddy,

Auntie Dolly took me to Hebrew School today. Mr. Klein is the teacher and he says he remembers Daddy when he was a little boy. I am the only girl in the class. We all sit around a big table and take turns reading. Mr. Klein was very pleased with me, as I remembered the Hebrew letters you taught me and it was really easy. I am going to go there three times a week.

I wish I could see you both and give you big hugs.

Lots of love,
Cynthia

I was surprised to find that I loved Hebrew school. Classes were held at the synagogue in a back room lined with dusty shelves holding tattered, musty-smelling holy books. I sounded out the curly Hebrew letters and memorized prayers with ease. Every morning, as soon as I got out of bed, I recited the morning prayer of thanks for another day of life, as Mr. Klein had taught us to do: "*Modeh anee lefanecha melech chai vekayam….*" *I thank you, living and eternal King….* I had no idea what it meant at the time, but even though I didn't understand the words, reciting the prayer gave me a feeling of rootedness, of being connected to something greater than myself.

The last time I'd encountered boys in a school setting had been in South Godstone and the Hebrew school boys were very different. Their parents were shopkeepers like mine. They didn't fight and swear like the South Godstone boys did so I felt quite comfortable around them, but they took no notice of me. They were scared of Mr. Klein who rapped them over the knuckles with a ruler if they dared misbehave or fidget. Their Hebrew reading was hesitant and sounded strange pronounced with a Welsh accent. Because I was such a good student, I felt very much at home in the dingy classroom, basking in Mr. Klein's praise.

> *Dear Mummy and Daddy,*
> *Auntie Dolly and I had a huge quarrel today. I wanted to wear my blue silk dress to Hebrew school. I love going there and I wanted to look nice. She said I could only wear it to parties. She said the classroom is dirty and the benches are full of splinters. I don't have any parties to go to here because my friends are all in Croydon so the dress just hangs in the wardrobe. I will grow out of it soon and it will hardly have been worn. She made me go upstairs to take it off but I crept up when she wasn't looking and put it back on. Mr. Klein said I looked really nice. When I got home, I tried to run upstairs to change, but Auntie Dolly heard me come in and she was really cross. She said I wasn't to write to you about this but I don't want to tell lies and not telling you would be almost like telling a lie.*
> *I love you both so much.*
>
> *Love,*
> *Cynthia*

On Sunday afternoons Dolly gave me sixpence—about $1.85 today—and I went to the run-down cinema where I would try to find a seat that wasn't broken. I'd never been to the movies by myself before. My mother's sisters Fan, Rose, and Milly took turns taking me to the cinema, vying for my attention. Alone in the rickety Merthyr movie house, I would lose myself in Hollywood movies like *Yankee Doodle Dandy, Going My Way* and *Cover Girl*, imagining myself joining Rita Hayworth and Bing Crosby to sing duets up there on the silver screen. "B" movies and newsreels always came before the main feature. The newsreels showed footage of D-Day and bombing raids by our brave RAF. They reminded me that the war still raged in Croydon and all over Europe, and I often had to hold back tears as I thought about my parents, who were still exposed to severe danger. During intermission, an usherette appeared under a spotlight at the front of the theater carrying a tray of ice cream cups, candy and cigarettes. I would buy my cup of ice cream and savor it during the main feature, licking the wooden spoon long after the ice cream was finished.

Once, Dolly took me to a meeting in the town hall which ended with the crowd singing "God Save the King." I was amazed when everyone around me then began singing the Welsh national anthem, *"Hen Wlad Fy Nhadau"* ("Land of My Fathers") in four-part harmony with a passion that had been missing from "God Save the King." It was the first time I'd ever stood in the midst of choral singers and, as I listened to the music around me, I felt goosebumps prickling my arms, even though I couldn't understand the words.

The future looked bleak. I'd finished all the school assignments and there would be no more Hebrew school until autumn. I wrapped my arms around myself in bed at night, trying to imagine my parents hugging me, and often cried myself to sleep. During the day, Dolly snapped at me just like she did at Grandpa, and I tried to stay out of her way. I longed for my parents.

Dearest Cynthia,

I went to a meeting at school today. The bomb damage is being repaired and classes will resume in the autumn.

I met with Miss Adams and she agreed to let you go to Worcester with a group of girls for the rest of the summer. Croydon High is going to take over a boarding school and arrange for recreational activities.

So pack your suitcase and get ready to come home for a couple of days to get ready for an exciting summer.

Lots of love,
Mummy

A summer holiday with my classmates would be a totally new experience. Boy Scouts and Girl Guides camped in tents for one or two weeks in the summer but Britain had no tradition of children going off to summer camp for extended stays as they did in the United States.

I was excited. But while I couldn't wait to leave Merthyr, I became terrified when Dolly told me I would have to travel back to London by myself.

"It's a long train ride," I said, worrying out loud at dinner that night.

Again Grandpa made fun of me.

"Sylvia could do it by herself, couldn't you Sylvia?" he croaked.

"Yeth," she said proudly. I glowered at the toddler across the table.

A few days before my departure, Grandpa surprised me by bringing home a present. I unwrapped the brown paper parcel and found a salmon-pink robe with ostrich feathers down the front and around the neck. I put it on and paraded in front of the mirror. It was a bit long—obviously a woman's size—and the smell of stale perfume clung to the feathers. It didn't occur to me to wonder where it had come from; I thought it looked glamorous. Dolly and Grandpa asked me to model it for them. I swished down the stairs, grasping the front so I wouldn't trip, and sashayed across the dining room.

"There's pretty you look," Dolly said. "What bewtiful taste your Grandpa has," she added, giving Grandpa a strange look.

Grandpa nodded and actually smiled under his nicotine-stained moustache. When Dolly packed my suitcase, she laid the robe carefully on top so it would be the first thing my mother saw when she unpacked.

Dolly took me to the station and found a maternal-looking woman who was also traveling to Cardiff and who agreed to see that I caught the London train safely. During the hour-long journey, I worried that my chaperone would get off the train at an earlier stop and I would have to change trains in Cardiff all by myself. I played the scene out in my mind, imagining myself lost in a huge crowd, getting on the wrong train and ending up somewhere in Scotland. But my fears were groundless. My companion kept her word and escorted me to the correct platform.

As I waited for the London train, I studied the tattered posters on the station walls. One in particular caught my attention. It showed a funny cartoon drawing of Hitler's face and head with one huge ear and read:

Careless Talk Costs Lives
Mr. Hitler Wants to Know!
He wants to know the unit's name
Where it's going – whence it came
Ships, guns and shells all make him curious
But silence makes him simply Fuehrious

Another poster featured an elderly cartoon couple and their dog standing in front of a ticket window. The caption asked: "Is Your Journey Really Necessary?" The point, I knew, was to discourage people from traveling for pleasure in order to leave valuable train seats for members of the armed services.

The train to London was so crowded, I wondered if anyone ever answered "no" to that question. Many travelers were indeed servicemen. One man wearing an army uniform limped into my compartment leaning on a cane. He sat down with one leg stuck out awkwardly in front of him and twisted a little to one side. I couldn't help staring at his deformity and kept sneaking glimpses until I became aware of a strange feeling that someone was looking at *me*. I glanced up and saw that he was glaring at me, his jaw thrust forward, his bloodshot eyes bulging. The hand not holding the cane was balled up into a fist. Traveling alone on the train, I was suddenly terrified. Was he going to stand up and hit me? My face flamed and my stomach jerked. How many times had my mother told me, "Don't stare, Cynthia. It's rude." I dropped my eyes quickly to the floor and studied the dirty cigarette butts people had ground out with their heels. I could still feel the soldier's gaze and was afraid to look up. His anger was a fitting climax to the misery I'd experienced in Merthyr.

When I got off the train in Paddington, I saw Mum at the end of the platform and we ran toward each other with outstretched arms. I had never been so happy to see her.

At home, she opened my suitcase and lifted out the salmon-colored, befeathered robe with the tips of her fingers as if it were a dirty handkerchief.

"What on earth is this?"

"It's a present from Grandpa."

"You can't wear it," she said.

"Why not? It's pretty!"

My mother blushed and frowned. "For one thing, it's not new, Cynthia. I suspect Grandpa got it from a lady friend."

"So? I like it!"

"It's not suitable for a young girl," my mother said firmly. She shook her head and let the robe drop to the floor. "What was Grandpa thinking?"

I didn't understand then that "lady friend" meant mistress. I didn't even know what a mistress was, much less that Grandpa's mistress was the local Madam of Merthyr. I was just disappointed. I loved the gentle caressing feel of the silky fabric and soft ostrich feathers and was sorry when the robe mysteriously disappeared.

Back in Croydon, the sirens wailed several times a day, and as soon as they were quiet the explosions began.

Mum and I had to quickly wash my clothes and repack my suitcase, for in two days, I would be going away again.

Chapter 24
Summer Vacation

Paddington Station was familiar terrain for me by now. A large group of girls, all wearing Croydon High School hats and blazers, was gathered by the information booth. I was 11 and most of them were around my age. Several teachers were with them: Miss Adams, our headmistress, short and plump with faded red hair; Miss Robertson, a history teacher, her head wrapped in a tiara of thick, blond braids; and Mrs. Puddicombe, a softer, prettier version of Miss Robertson. I learned later she was Miss Robertson's sister. My heart sank when I saw Miss Mounsey, my least favorite teacher in the whole school, standing off to one side, one hand characteristically placed just below her throat, playing with her string of beads. I decided to stay as far away from her as I could. What kind of a summer holiday was this going to be with Miss Mounsey joining us?

Miss Adams' Scottish burr sounded more shrill than usual as she shouted to be heard over the rattle and roar of trains and broadcast announcements.

"Now Gurrls!" she began. "You are off to a great summer adventure. Remember that you are guests of the Alice Ottley School. Their teachers will be leading many of your activities so please be appreciative and thank them graciously for their help. When you get back in September, the school's bomb damage will have been repaired and you can look forward to a wonderful year ahead." She drew back her shoulders. "And now, gurrls," she continued, "Three cheers for the school! Hip hip…"

"Hurray!" we responded in loud unison, repeating the cheer three times.

The Alice Ottley School was in Worcester, in the Midlands northwest of London, far away from air raids and Doodlebugs. News of the bomb damage to our school had apparently spread through the private school grapevine; such events were only vaguely reported on the news. When Miss Roden, the headmistress of the Alice Ottley School, heard of it, she had phoned Miss Adams and suggested that a group of Croydon girls come and stay for the summer. Together, the two headmistresses had swiftly recruited a team of teachers from both schools to run a program of camp-like activities.

Because resources and staff were limited, Miss Adams could take only about 40 girls, and admission was restricted to those who had no alternative place to go to escape the Doodlebugs. When my mother asked that I be included, Miss Adams remembered that I was staying with my grandfather and said no. My mother pleaded, telling Miss Adams how miserable I was in Wales. I don't know what she said, but she was persuasive and Miss Adams finally relented.

We hugged our mothers, said our goodbyes, piled into the train and put our suitcases up on the luggage racks. We were all excited about the adventure ahead. We wondered if our boarding school would be like the schools Angela Brazil and Enid Blyton wrote about in their novels. We all loved their books.

After a three-hour train journey and a long walk from Worcester's Foregate Station, we arrived at the Alice Ottley School. We were so tired that we went to bed straight after tea. But, tired as I was, I found it hard to fall asleep. I was sharing a dormitory room with seven other girls, and their heavy breathing and occasional snores kept me awake as I was unaccustomed to sharing a bedroom. As the long

English twilight dimmed into darkness, I stared up at the ceiling, thinking about the sirens and explosions we'd left behind.

The next day, we explored the building, a grand mansion boasting three staircases which had once been a private residence. One staircase with narrow, splintery stairs leading down to the kitchen area had obviously been for servants. Another formal staircase took us to the entrance hall, its banister beautifully carved and ending with an elegant curve. I imagined descending it on my way to a formal ball, wearing glittering jewels and an elegant evening gown. The third staircase led down to a space behind the main-floor living area. I was constantly confused by the staircases and always seemed to take the wrong one, so I spent a lot of time getting lost in the rambling building.

Although I didn't love the idea of sharing a bedroom, we were all excited to be sleeping in a real dormitory with narrow beds lined up on two sides of the room—just like the dormitories we read about in novels—and we chattered late into the night. We shared our fears for the parents we'd left behind, and this led to an epidemic of homesickness that ran through the group like a virus. One of the girls, Jennifer Swann, would sit cross-legged on her bed every evening, brushing her long, shiny brown hair and sobbing, her sobs matching the rhythm of her brushstrokes. Every night, I read another chapter of *Lassie Come Home* before I went to sleep, the words blurring as I wept all through the story. Sometimes, I wasn't sure if my sadness was because of the brave lost dog trying to find her way back home or because of the nagging worry about my parents' safety.

Teachers from Alice Ottley helped with many of our planned activities. Worcester Cathedral towered over the town, and we were taken on a tour. Although the heat that day was sweltering, the air inside the cathedral felt almost cold. The most exciting part of the tour was a demonstration of the organ given by the choir master and organist, Sir Ivor Atkins. The organ loft floor trembled under our feet as he played and showed us how incredibly complicated it was to coordinate hands and feet and pull out stops. I had started taking piano lessons on the piano my father bought while my mother and I were living in South Godstone, and I found playing with two hands enough of a challenge. I knew I would never be able to play an organ.

After the organ demonstration, a deacon led us up to the tower. The first flight of stairs was easy, but as we climbed higher the spiral stairs became very steep. There was no banister and the narrow, pie-wedge-shaped steps were treacherous. I thought they had been designed for tiny medieval feet, not for my size nines. I hoped to see a doorway around every corner but there were only more stairs—more than two hundred of them, ending in the bell tower. From that high aerie we could see far, far away, beyond the city to bucolic farmland dotted with cows and sheep. Swans looked like white pinpricks on the River Severn, and people were tiny toys.

On another day, we took a bus to Droitwich Spa, a charming town with shops housed in old Tudor buildings. There, we swam in a saltwater pool fed by hot springs where steam rose from the water and filled the air with strange, sulphury smells. Teachers led us on hikes along the banks of the River Severn and we picnicked on blankets spread on the grass. On one hot afternoon, we went to an orchard to pick plums. The farmer shook the trees and plums fell onto tarpaulin sheets spread below. I picked five bushel baskets, some girls picked more, and we snacked on Victoria plums until the juice ran down our chins. We were a little disappointed to be served two plums for tea when we got back to the school and I fell asleep to the sound of groans from girls who had overindulged.

To my great relief, Miss Mounsey didn't supervise any activities. She had come to Worcester to be our cook. Who would have guessed that my nemesis could prepare quite tasty lunches and elegant tea sandwiches? Still, I avoided her, afraid she would criticize something I wore or my boisterous behavior. One Sunday morning, the other girls and teachers went to worship in Worcester Cathedral and Miss Mounsey stayed behind to prepare lunch. I was the only Jewish girl in the Worcester program and was exempt from attending church services. I was surprised when Miss Mounsey poked her head around the door to the sitting room where I was reading and asked, "Would you like to help me make lunch?"

I closed my book and followed her into the sunny kitchen where a long butcher-block table ran almost the length of the room. Though I would have been quite capable of helping in the kitchen at home, my mother had never encouraged me to do so. She usually told me to keep out of her way.

"We have to cut up a lot of cabbage for salad," Miss Mounsey said. She showed me how to curl my fingers back to keep them out of the way of the very sharp knife she entrusted me with, and I sliced cabbage paper thin, exactly the way she had demonstrated. When she started to throw the cabbage core away, I had the temerity to say, "Don't do that, Miss Mounsey. It's the best part. My mummy says it's as good as an apple."

"Well, goodness me, you're right," she said as we both munched on cabbage stumps. At lunch that day, Miss Mounsey announced to the girls assembled in the dining room: "This salad was beautifully prepared by Cynthia Shelower." I blushed with pride and our relationship changed. From then on, when Miss Mounsey and I met in the school hallways, she always greeted me with a warm smile that I happily returned.

A universal feature of life at the girls' boarding schools we read about in novels was the midnight feast, when girls would filch food from the kitchen, hide it under their beds and wake up in the middle of the night to gorge on forbidden treats. Some of us were determined to live out this fantasy and there was much whispering about how and when we would conduct our escapade.

A day or so after we began planning, Miss Robertson gathered us together in the sitting room and announced, "Those girls who would like to have a midnight feast will do so on the Saturday night before we travel back to Croydon."

It took the wind out of our sails a little to learn that our plans had been discovered. Would a midnight feast be exciting if the teachers knew we were holding it? We weren't sure. Still, we decided to go ahead.

Another British boarding school tradition was the tuck box, a box packed with snacks and treats parents purchased for their children to take with them to school. Many of the other girls' parents had used their own candy rations to buy sweets for their daughters. My parents, with an eye to good nutrition, had added walnuts, a nutcracker and dried fruit. Walnuts were a luxury and I had decided to save them to share with my friends.

On the appointed night, five of us set our alarms for midnight. Rudely awakened, we staggered out of bed, groggily pulled a selection of chocolate bars, hard candies and my fruit and nuts out of our tuck boxes, then tiptoed out to the hallway, filed into a walk-in closet and spread everything out on the floor. We sat giggling and whispering and plowed our way through the food even though we weren't hungry. We all felt weird afterwards, not being accustomed to stuffing ourselves with sweets in the middle of the night, and decided that midnight feasts were greatly overrated.

At the beginning of September, we traveled back to Croydon. The repairs to Croydon High were not yet completed so I was left to my own devices at home while my mother was at work. She would make me a sandwich for lunch before she left in the morning, and I occupied myself with dolls, books, coloring and drawing until she returned.

Doodlebugs had been replaced by now with an even more terrifying weapon: the V-2 rocket. V-2s flew higher, faster and farther than V-1s and were completely silent, giving no warning of their approach. They were much more destructive, carrying ten tons of explosive, and when they hit the ground the sound could be heard from as much as 20 miles away. Because they traveled greater distances from their launch points than the V-1s did, very few of them dropped on Croydon, landing instead in North London and beyond.

On the evening of October 26, 1944, a V-2 landed on Palmers Green railroad station, at the end of Bubbe's street. The blast from the explosion caused her kitchen cabinet to fall on her. A pot flew out, hitting her right eye and blinding it completely. Fortunately she wasn't killed and the house wasn't destroyed. When the district nurse came to the house to evaluate Bubbe's injuries, she also diagnosed diabetes. Although Bubbe had probably been diabetic for a long time, my family believed the shock of the bombing had caused her illness and considered Bubbe a victim of Hitler's bombing campaigns.

Bubbe already had a cataract in her left eye so she had very little vision left, but she never lost her sense of humor. After the accident she would joke that "I'm blind in one eye and can't see out of the other one," and laughter would ripple through her ample body.

The V-2 rockets were Hitler's last effort to break the spirits of the British people. He failed. The rockets traveled too high and fast to be shot down. The only way to stop them was for Allied troops to gain control of their launching sites in Holland and destroy them on the ground. Gradually, through the rest of the year, the strikes began tapering off as the Allies advanced through Europe. Grownups said the end of the war was in sight. We waited anxiously for peace.

Published by GRAHAM & GILLIES LTD., Shell Mex House, Strand

Cynthia Ehrenkrantz

Chapter 25
Dancing in the Street

On April 13, 1945, my twelfth birthday, my mother roused me for school.

"Happy birthday, darling. It's nearly eight o'clock. You're going to be late for school."

As usual, my mother was lying about the time. It was really just 7.30, but in my early morning groggy state I always believed her and staggered out of bed to the bathroom and then to the kitchen where a bowl of cornflakes and a cup of tea were waiting on the table. A messy eater, I always ate breakfast before dressing, not wanting to drip milk down my school uniform.

My mother sat down next to me.

"I have a special present for you," she said. "What have you always wished for on your birthday candles?"

"A baby brother or sister," I replied with a shrug.

"Well. It looks as if you're going to get your wish," she said. "I'm going to have a baby."

My jaw dropped and my sleepy eyes widened. "A baby!" I squealed. "Ooh, Mummy! How wonderful! When? How soon?"

"Not until October," she said. "Now don't tell anyone. It's still a secret, just between you, me and Daddy." She smiled. "This baby is really for you," she continued. "You've always begged for a brother or sister. Now you'll have one at last."

Yes. I had longed for a brother or sister for as long as I could remember for purely selfish reasons. I'd noticed that the most popular girls at school usually had siblings and that "only" children like me were generally a little odd. Of course, I wanted to be popular. Perhaps a baby in our family would open a pathway to the popularity I longed for.

I didn't know it at the time but my mother had miscarried several times since having me. When war broke out, my parents had stopped thinking about more children, but as the Allies advanced after D-Day and it became clear that the war was winding down and we would be victorious, they started planning for the future again. My father had decided to start a new business. Many buildings had been destroyed in air raids; countless others had sustained damage. He planned to become a licensed building contractor, purchase the damaged buildings, repair them and sell them at a profit. The world would be peaceful at last and he would make a good living. Optimistic about the future, my parents decided to try to have another child.

No bombs had fallen on Croydon in more than a month. The skies over all of Britain were newly quiet. We were all saddened by the news of President Roosevelt's sudden death, but we still had Mr. Churchill to lead us, and our little family was suffused with joy at the prospect of a new baby.

Then, on April 30, 1945, Adolph Hitler killed himself in a bunker in Berlin. A week later, the Nazis surrendered to the Allies, and on May 8, 1945, the war in Europe ended. V-E Day.

"Let me get you a cup of tea, Till," my father said, his hand resting lightly on my mother's shoulder. "Shall I make you a sandwich? You're eating for two now." We had gathered in the kitchen to hear the 3:00 p.m. broadcast of Mr. Churchill's victory speech from a balcony of the Ministry of Health building in Whitehall.

"This is your victory," Churchill said to the thousands of people gathered below. "Victory of the cause of freedom in every land. In all our long history, we have never seen a greater day than this."

I watched tears well up in Mummy's eyes as my father grasped her hand.

"Everyone, man or woman, has done their best," Churchill continued. "Everyone has tried, none have flinched. Neither the long years, nor the dangers, nor the fierce attacks of the enemy, have in any way weakened the unbending resolve of the British nation. God bless you all."

When the Prime Minister finished speaking, the crowd cheered wildly and the three of us stood and hugged. My parents, wreathed in smiles, spun around as they embraced. I had thought nothing could make me happier than my mother's news about the coming baby, but I was wrong. At last, the war had ended.

Bells began ringing in St. Mildred's Church and Our Lady of the Annunciation a few blocks away. I couldn't remember ever hearing church bells before. They'd been banned during the war and would only toll, we had been told, to warn us of imminent invasion. Now they rang out in joy.

After a supper of salad sprinkled with grated cheddar cheese, we waited through the long twilight. Finally, when it was getting dark, my parents and I joined crowds of people walking into town under a sky criss-crossed with searchlights tracing V-for-Victory patterns against the blackness. British, American and Russian flags fluttered above us from grimy, war-damaged buildings, their broken windows boarded up or covered with black paper.

Hundreds of people had gathered around a huge bonfire outside the town hall, many of them waving Union Jacks. Scratchy gramophone recordings played patriotic songs over a loudspeaker: "There'll Always Be an England," "The White Cliffs of Dover" and "When They Sound the Last 'All Clear.'" We all joined in, singing at the tops of our voices. Small boys climbed to the top of the Cenotaph, Croydon's memorial to victims of the First World War, to get a better view, and we cheered and shouted as a straw-stuffed figure of Hitler, complete with a black cowlick falling over his forehead and a little black moustache, was cast into the bonfire's flames. My parents held hands as they watched me dance around the fire. Strangers threw their arms around each other. I yelled "Hurray! Hurray!" till I was hoarse and could shout no more.

At ten o'clock, people rolled out of the pubs and the stale smell of beer filled the air as they danced and sang "Knees Up Mother Brown" and "Hands Knees and Boomps-a-Daisy." My mother frowned in disapproval as the energetic dancing to "Knees Up" gave us glimpses of women's underwear and the "Boomps-a-Daisy" dancers banged their behinds together in every chorus. "Such vulgar dances," my mother said. But everyone looked as if they were having such a good time. Who cared if they were vulgar? I thought. Blackout curtains had been pulled aside and light shone from windows all the way home as I ran ahead of my parents back to our house.

Chapter 26
New Beginnings

Two weeks later, we heard that a general election would be held for the first time since before the war began. Election Day was set for July 5 but the results wouldn't be announced until the end of the month to allow time for late voting in some areas and for ballots cast by servicemen overseas to be collected and counted.

Throughout the war, we'd been governed by a coalition government of Conservative, Liberal and Labour party leaders headed by Winston Churchill. They had guided us through evacuation programs, the Blitz, Doodlebugs and rationing without any public hint of party disagreements. Conservative party leader Winston Churchill, with his bulldog ugliness and stubby cigar, had become a symbol of the country's plucky patriotism, traveling the country to inspect bomb sites, meeting with dignitaries in the zippered onesie called a siren suit he had designed himself so it could be donned quickly during air raids; always flashing his two-fingered V-for-Victory sign to crowds and cameras; rallying the government and people after Dunkirk with his vow that "we shall defend our island whatever the cost may be, we shall fight on the beaches…we shall fight in the hills; we shall never surrender…." It looked as if his re-election was assured.

One day at school in early June, after the six other Jewish girls and I had filed into the assembly hall to hear the day's announcements, Miss Adams walked to the podium in her flowing academic robes and said she had special news.

"Now that there's going to be the first general election in ten years," she said, "we will hold a mock election here in school. You will select girls as candidates, set out party platforms and hold political rallies. Your classroom teachers will instruct you about rules to be followed."

We marched out of the hall to the rousing sound of "Rule, Britannia!" pounded out on the piano by Miss Braggins, the music teacher.

Miss Rolfe, our homeroom teacher, was already in front of the blackboard when we got back to our classroom, tendrils of dark blond hair escaping from her bun. She told us the election would be conducted in true British Public School style.

The political parties would be the same as those in the national election and mirror their policies. The left-leaning Labour party promised to enact a host of new social welfare programs proposed in a seminal 1942 paper known as *The Beveridge Report*. The right-leaning Conservatives, Mr. Churchill's party, took credit for endorsing free secondary education for all, but otherwise stood for fiscal restraint and slower social change. The Liberals boasted that Sir William Beveridge, author of *The Beveridge Report*, belonged to their party but they didn't have much else to say for themselves.

"You are encouraged to make posters supporting your candidates and their policies," Miss Rolfe said. "Of course, there will be no writing on walls and you may not pull down your opponents' posters or write on them. When you hold meetings, you should feel free to ask questions but there will be absolutely no booing or shouting at candidates when they're speaking."

Most of my school friends were upper-middle class girls whose fathers practiced law or medicine or were engaged in other professions. My father was in trade. Most of my classmates embraced their parents' political opinions. Some older girls had formed their own independent views but the younger ones parroted what they heard at home. I suppose I did too.

I regarded my father with some awe. He'd fought fires during the Blitz and flying bomb attacks, and when he was out of uniform he sported a red tie to advertise his left-wing Labour Party affiliation. Between fires, fire stations can be boring places and the men tried to fill time in meaningful ways. My father was in charge of the education program at his fire station and often invited guest speakers to present their visions of the new world that would rise from the ashes after the war. Many of them quoted from *The Beveridge Report* and discussed what it identified as "five giants on the road of reconstruction": Want, Disease, Ignorance, Squalor and Idleness.

At suppertime Daddy would tell us about the speakers and discussions.

"The chaps at the fire station don't want to go back to the way things were before the war," he said one evening. "You mark my words. If Labour gets elected, things are going to change." My parents planned to vote Labour in the general election. Labour was the party of workers, not elites. When it came time to choose a party for the mock election at school, I chose Labour. It was the right party for me.

So many girls joined the Conservatives, they had to meet in the gym. The two smaller parties caucused in classrooms. There were just six girls of my Labour persuasion, though it looked as if about 30 girls would vote Liberal. Posters began appearing on walls with the slogans "Labour for Homes" and "Labour for Security" and from the Conservative party, "Demand Democracy, Not Bureaucracy." Discussions at recess became heated.

"Of course, we should vote for Mr. Churchill," my friend Margaret said. "He led us through the war and we should vote for him out of gratitude."

"But he wants to go back to the way things were before the war," I argued. "Men coming home need decent housing and health care."

"Oh, they won't know what to do with decent housing," she retorted. "Everyone knows when working class people get bath tubs they fill them with coal."

We held our school election two weeks before the country went to the polls. When the count was in, our little Labour party was gratified to see that we'd gleaned 12 votes: twice what we'd anticipated.

The Croydon High School Conservatives of course won by a landslide. While etiquette had been mandatory for the period before the election, no one had told the Tories that gloating was taboo. After their candidate delivered her victory speech, they lorded it over us and we didn't know how to respond.

"Our school election is just a forecast of how things are going to turn out in the whole country," Margaret said as we sat at the lunch table eating carrot buns. "Everyone loves Mr. Churchill. He's sure to be elected."

But I thought about the campaign speech he'd given some weeks before that my mother and I had listened to together:

"I must tell you that a socialist policy is abhorrent to British ideas on freedom," Mr. Churchill had intoned, then had gone on to warn that if the Labour Party won, a socialist state would soon control every aspect of people's lives: "where they are to work… where they may go and what they may say, what views they are to hold… and what education their children are to receive." Inevitably, he predicted, a socialist Labour government would establish some form of political police to suppress dissent and opposition. "They would have to fall back on some form of Gestapo," Mr. Churchill said.

He was slurring his words. "He's drunk," my mother said, wrinkling her nose in distaste.

Mr. Churchill apparently did his party no favors with that kind of fear-mongering. Election results were announced on July 26, 1945. Labour won by a landslide, gaining 239 seats in Parliament for a total of 393 members, while the Conservatives lost almost half their seats, dropping from 387 to 197. Mr. Churchill tendered his resignation as Prime Minister that same day, and Clement Attlee, head of the Labour Party, took his place. It was our turn now to gloat over the Conservative girls at school. They were totally bewildered by the election results and at lunch time they wagged their heads and talked about "the ruination of the country."

The war with Japan continued, but that was America's war. British servicemen fought the Japanese alongside the Yanks, but Germany had been our personal enemy. They'd dropped bombs on us and we were just learning about the unspeakable horrors of concentration camps: Auschwitz, Bergen-Belsen, Buchenwald, Dachau. V-E Day had meant we would have peace at last. The war in the Pacific seemed far away.

Eleven days after the election results were announced, the U.S. dropped an atomic bomb on Hiroshima; three days later it dropped another on Nagasaki. The *Daily Mail* ran a picture of the first mushroom cloud on its front page. Japan surrendered on August 15: V-J Day. We rejoiced again. The entire war was now officially over.

My brother, Robert, was born on October 3, 1945. The maternity hospital was next door to Croydon High School. The day after he was born, my friends and I climbed the school fire escape during our lunch hour. My mother came to the hospital window across from us and waved as a nurse held the baby up for us to admire, his wrinkled red face framed by a blanket. He bore a strong resemblance to Winston Churchill.

I was the center of attention in the classroom and at lunchtime for the next few days. I had to share my parents' attention when my mother brought Robert home, but I didn't mind. The war was over, Labour was in power and, at school, I basked in the glory of having a real baby brother. The world had changed for the better, our family was safe and happy and, finally, I was one of the popular girls.

Carrot Buns
- 8 ounces self-rising flour
- 3 ounces margarine
- 3 ounces sugar
- 4 tablespoons finely grated raw carrot
- 2 ounces raisins
- 1 reconstituted dried egg
- A little milk or water

1. Preheat oven to 425 degrees.
2. Grease a cookie sheet and set aside.
3. Sift the flour into a mixing bowl, then rub in the margarine with your fingers until crumbs form.
4. Add sugar, carrot, raisins and egg. Mix well, then add sufficient milk or water to make a sticky dough.
5. Divide mixture into 12 small heaps on cookie sheet and bake 12-15 minutes until firm and golden.

Epilogue
Child of War

In the autumn of 1945, Bubbe found out why letters and strings of dried mushrooms had stopped arriving from her family in Poland. Most of her relatives, including her father, her sister and brothers, her siblings' spouses and most of their children, had died in Auschwitz. Six were sent to the gas chamber the day before the camp was liberated. Only two nephews—her sister Hannah's son, Sam Tremback, and her brother Issy's son, Morry Krycer—survived. They were put in a Displaced Persons' camp and were horrified to discover that General George S. Patton, a known anti-Semite, had surrounded the camp with barbed wire and hired SS soldiers and concentration camp guards to help operate and patrol it. The survivors were not supposed to leave but one night Sam and Morry escaped by crawling under a fence. Somehow, they remembered Bubbe's address and wrote to Uncle Goody asking if they could come to London to join the family. He tried to get papers for them, but Britain would not issue visas – not even for a visit. So Uncle Goody dipped into his savings and bought them passages to Australia where we had other relatives. He traveled to Paris to meet them, gave them their tickets and saw them to the train which would take them to their ship. Some months later, Bubbe and Uncle Goody received letters from Sam and Morry saying they had successfully established themselves Down Under, on the other side of the world.

Bubbe never stopped grieving for her other lost family members. On Saturday afternoons, I watched her leaf through old photo albums, gazing with dimmed vision at pictures they had sent before the war, her tears blotching the snapshots.

The elation we felt in Britain on VE Day quickly evaporated. Postwar austerity was, in many ways, worse than the deprivations suffered in wartime. The United States abruptly terminated the Lend-Lease program that had supplied us with certain basics, and the country was unable to pivot quickly from a war footing to peacetime food production and imports. Instead of ending when the war was over, rationing became more stringent.

Throughout the war, we had been told not to waste bread. Although we all despised the National Loaf, it had been cheap, nutritious, readily available and never rationed. Then, in July 1946, bread was suddenly rationed and we all regarded this as the greatest insult. The following year, the potato crop failed and stockpiles were ruined by frost, and in November 1947 even potatoes, our staple throughout the war, were rationed.

Walking through London's West End, my mother and I would gaze with envy into department store windows displaying washing machines, refrigerators and electric mixers—all labeled "For Export Only." The economy was in terrible shape and the government was in dire need of foreign currency. British citizens weren't allowed to buy these luxuries, and few could afford them.

So many buildings had been bombed that thousands of people were without permanent housing. Married children moved in with their parents and families went on long waiting lists for public housing. I didn't see my first "For Rent" and "For Sale" signs on houses and apartments until I came to the U.S. in 1957. I have no memory of ever seeing such signs in England.

The one bright spot after the war was the National Health Services, established in July 1948. Health care for all was a dream come true. Although Britons were heavily taxed in order to pay for it, people didn't complain because the benefit of the NHS—granting equal access to health care regardless of income, employment or status – was so great.

My father grudgingly praised the Health Service, but he soon became frustrated with the slow pace of social progress. Eventually, he turned his back on his socialist ideals and railed against the Labour government. In the next general election, he switched to voting Conservative. As I matured into a young woman, I leaned further and further to the left and my father and I argued constantly about politics.

Ironically, the war was the high point of my parents' marriage. While my father was a fireman, money was rarely an issue. My parents had no money but neither did anyone else. The new business he started after the war—repairing and renovating war-damaged houses—should have thrived in the housing shortage. But he was such a bad money manager that the business failed, and he declared bankruptcy in 1949, owing money to friends and family.

After the business failed, my parents sold our house in Croydon and we moved to Kentish Town, a working-class neighborhood in northwest London. My parents now quarreled about money all the time, my mother weeping and my father descending into uncontrollable rages. My mother hated owing money to anyone. My father didn't believe in paying bills till they were long overdue, if at all. In 1952, when I was 19 and my brother, Robert, was seven, they divorced and my father disappeared. Years later, when I was married and had children of my own, I decided to try to find him. He had three grandchildren he'd never met, and I thought his temper might have mellowed with age. I didn't know if he was still living so I visited the General Register Office in London where all records of births and deaths were kept, entered into huge ledgers in Copperplate script. His name jumped off the page: Max Harriss Shelower. He had died in North London in March, 1977, just before his 70th birthday.

When newsreels began showing footage of the death camps and the living skeletons who were survivors, I was horrified and shaken and began having nightmares about our own family members' suffering and deaths.

My commitment to Judaism was deepened. I joined Habonim, a Socialist Zionist youth movement, and planned to emigrate to Palestine and live out my Socialist ideals on a kibbutz. I believed that, with the establishment of a Jewish state, anti-Semitism would be eliminated forever. In 1950, when I was 17 and the State of Israel was just two years old, I attended a year-long program in Israel that brought youth leaders together from all over the world to live, work and study in the brand new Jewish State. We were a fiercely idealistic bunch from mixed backgrounds: some of us had survived concentration camps; others were from affluent homes. In the course of a few weeks, Hebrew became our lingua franca and we formed a community.

Living for part of that year on an Israeli kibbutz, I found my strong Socialist beliefs put to the test. I worked hard in the fields and the kitchen, receiving no remuneration but the knowledge that I was contributing to the good of the kibbutz and the country.

The years 1950-51 were a time of great austerity in Israel, caused in part by mass immigration that doubled the population in three years. Food and consumer goods were in short supply, so I was thrust back into the wartime mode of material deprivation. But there was a joyful idealism in the young country that gave the sacrifices we were all making a special kind of infectious energy. Back in England, in return for the scholarship, I recommitted myself to the youth movement and planned to return to Israel as soon as possible to live permanently on a kibbutz. Those plans were postponed when my mother became ill and needed surgery and home care. They changed completely after I met my future husband.

I was working in the advertising department of *The New Statesman & Nation*, a socialist weekly journal, at the time. Ezra Ehrenkrantz was a young American architect in England on a Fulbright grant, developing a system for standardizing building components. His first Fulbright was followed by a second. Between his studies and research and my job and caretaking duties, we made time to fall in love. After two years in England, he returned to the U.S. to begin his military service as a commissioned officer in the army. His marriage proposal came by transatlantic telephone call in September 1956. On April 4, 1957, I arrived in New York on the *Queen Elizabeth* and descended the gangplank into the arms of my waiting fiancé, smiling and handsome in his uniform. We were married nine days later.

It was a time of great prosperity in America, a stark contrast to the still-struggling economy in Britain. I marveled at the huge portions of food my mother-in-law put on our plates and her constant encouragement to have second and third helpings. In my head, I could still hear my mother admonishing my father and me when we dared to ask for more, saying, "There's enough there for another meal y'know."

When Ezra finished his military service, we moved from Aberdeen, Maryland to Berkeley, California, where he began teaching in the architecture department at UC Berkeley. I had quit school and trained as a secretary when my father's business failed, because my parents could no longer afford the school fees, so I had never attended college. Ezra encouraged me to enroll at the university where I began studying anthropology. The experience opened a new, exciting world to me. In the American educational system, I encountered no barriers of class distinction as I would have in Britain. It gave me an appreciation for what it meant to be living in the Land of Opportunity.

More than 80 years have passed since Britain declared war on Germany, yet my early experiences during the war years still lurk inside me. Walking through an industrialized area of Cincinnati in 2019, I was startled by the deafening sound of the lunchtime factory siren. I gasped and covered my ears as my stomach jumped up toward my mouth and I was transformed into my seven-year-old self, terrified by the air-raid warning.

I never throw food away. I stow vegetable trimmings in the freezer to make stock. Limp vegetables and leftovers get dumped into a pot with a few herbs and a potato to make "refrigerator soup." I tear up old bedsheets to use as cleaning rags, for I never saw a paper towel until I came to the U.S.; they still seem like an extravagance. And when I read about children being separated from their parents at our southern border, I swallow my tears as I am thrust back into those months I spent in Merthyr living with strange, distant relatives and experiencing gut-wrenching longing for my parents.

While such memories bring back wartime hardships, some experiences influenced me positively. In South Godstone, wildflowers blossomed all around us: carpets of bluebells in the woods, wild primroses and sweet-smelling violets. I was enchanted by a neighbor's garden where flowers tumbled over walls and climbed up fences and the scent of lavender filled the air. I was only eight years old, but the memory of that garden stays with me. Having my own little garden patch in South Godstone gave me an appreciation of growing things and, particularly, a lifelong love of flowers. I still enjoy getting my hands in the dirt, watching buds swell and bloom, and I am a glutton for garden tours. A beautiful garden gives me as much pleasure as a great poem or piece of music. So for that legacy I am thankful.

Our wartime food challenges also instilled in me a lifelong interest in food: its preparation, literature and traditions. My professional life was spent in the gourmet food industry. I owned two specialty food stores and established my own wholesale company. The seeds of my food interests were firmly planted when every apple, every cabbage was precious.

During World War II in Britain, our enemy was clearly identified. We could direct our hatred at Adolf Hitler, the ludicrous, dangerous little man with the black moustache and a cowlick over his forehead. It gave us a huge feeling of unity. And we had Winston Churchill, whose plain-spoken oratory and honesty about the enemy threatening our shores inspired us to be brave and to develop the stiff upper lip that became such a well-known part of being British.

As I write these words, my adopted and much beloved country is deeply divided by a number of issues—social and political, domestic and international—and I find myself longing for the feeling of unity everyone shared in wartime Britain. We believed if we were united we could get through the toughest challenges. We were right about that.

We also believed despotism and brutality would die with Hitler, but now we've seen that this is not so.

My childhood wartime experiences were painful, but they were nothing compared to the hardships experienced by thousands of British children who were shunted from city to countryside and back again in an effort to keep them safe, or the unimaginable horrors inflicted on millions of children in Nazi-controlled Europe and the death camps.

Today, children all over the world are still forced to endure the suffering and privations of war, persecution, famine and climate-related disasters—all of it far worse than anything I ever knew. I grieve for them. My fervent wish is that they find safety, as I did, and be allowed to grow into adulthood in a peaceful world.

Acknowledgments

So many people have helped me on this journey, which has lasted more years than I care to count.

My first thanks go to my parents, Tilly and Max Shelower. Their love and resourcefulness sustained me through the war years and helped to give me resilience, for which I am deeply grateful.

Many thanks to Charles Salzberg, who insisted that I had a book to write, not just a hodge-podge of childhood memories. He inspired me to shape random musings into a story.

Deep appreciation also to members of my writing community: Cathleen Barnhart, Cindy Dircks, Terri Campion, Karen Gershowitz, Coree Spencer, Carol Hymowitz, Jack Eppler, Liz Tingley, Liz Burk, Phyllis Melhado, Fredricka Maister, Wendy Davis and Judy Rabinor. You all read many revisions with patience and offered ideas, encouragement and wisdom.

Thanks too to Fran Cook and the office staff of Croydon High School who gave me access to archives and welcomed me so warmly back to my old school. Thanks also to the staff of Croydon Public Library, who gave me so much help in researching the war years in Croydon.

I am grateful also to Lisa Romeo and Gini Kopecky Wallace, editors who helped shape my work with deep perception and constructive suggestions. This book owes so much to their expertise, and to Paula Markowitz Wittlin photographer par excellence.

To my children: Ruth, Dan and Jonathan. Your life and growth have brought me incalculable joy.

About the Author

Author Photo Credit: © Paula Markowitz Wittlin

Crawling on the floor to pick up pins with a u-shaped magnet in her Uncle Goody's tailoring and furrier shop in North London inspired Cynthia Ehrenkrantz to write *The Pinn Family Chronicles* when she was eight years old—a story about a family of pins living between the floorboards of a dressmaker's shop. She has been writing ever since but began publishing only more recently, after raising three children and retiring from a successful career in the food industry as founder and owner of two specialty food stores and a wholesale food brokerage company. Her work has since appeared in *Gourmet News Magazine, Simple Cooking, How Not to Greet Famous People: The Best Stories from ducts.org, riverSedge: a Journal of Art and Literature* and *Jewish Post & News.* A resident of White Plains, NY, she also performs her work at regional storytelling events and sings with the Yiddish Philharmonic Chorus. *Seeking Shelter* is her first published book. Learn more at **cynthiaehrenkrantz.com**.

Made in the USA
Middletown, DE
09 February 2023

23598216R00136